THE PILIPINOS IN AMERICA

Macro/Micro Dimensions of Immigration and Integration

THE PILIPINOS IN AMERICA

Macro/Micro Dimensions of Immigration and Integration

Antonio J.A. Pido

1986
Center for Migration Studies
New York

THE PILIPINOS IN AMERICA
Macro/Micro Dimensions of Immigration and Integration

First Edition
Copyright 1985 by
The Center for Migration Studies of New York, Inc.
All rights reserved. No part of this book may be reproduced
without permission from the author.

CENTER FOR MIGRATION STUDIES
209 Flagg Place • Staten Island • New York 10304

Library of Congress Cataloging in Publication Data

Pido, Antonio J.A., 1934-
The Pilipinos in America

Bibliography: p. 150 includes index

1. Pilipino Americans   I. Title
E184.F4P53 1985   973'.049921   85-47920
Library of Congress Catalog Number 85-047920
ISBN 0-913256-78-1 (Cloth)   0-913256-83-8 (Paper)
Printed in the United States of America

CONTENTS

LIST OF TABLES

Ruth H.
personal reiteration
of my sincere appreciation
cited below & warmest
regards
Tom 4/15/86

Acknowledgements

Rarely has any writer succeeded in getting his or her work published without the help of many others. This one is no exception. Assistance was provided by individuals and agencies (government and non-government) both in the Philippines and the United States and are acknowledged elsewhere as their contributions are mentioned in this work. Many others - researchers, librarians and colleagues - provided valuable information, criticisms and encouragement. To them, I am very grateful.

There are some who should be mentioned. They include: Professors John Useem, Ruth Hill Useem and Ruth S. Hamilton, Michigan State University, for providing the original ideas for this research, as well as their critical suggestions and encouragement; and to Dr. Lydia A. Beltran, Michigan Education Association and Ms. Rhea E. Lodge, Michigan Department of Labor for their valuable suggestions and editing assistance. I am, however, most grateful to the Center for Migration Studies (CMS) and its officials for publishing this work, including; the CMS reviewer who, because of editorial policies, may remain anonymous; and Ms. Barbara Costello and Ms. Eileen Reiter for their reviews, editing and suggestions.

Last but not least, I am grateful to my family for their moral and material support; my parents Pablo T. Pido and Luisa Alvarez Pido, my wife Maria Theresa and our children.

1. *Introduction*

ISSUES AND PERSPECTIVES

Until recently, most studies on U.S. majority-minority relations, particularly those concerned with the immigration experience, have used a structural functional approach based on an order-consensus model of society. The model assumed that the dominant Anglo Saxon society established by the first immigrants is the ideal world social order, and as such should also be the idealized social order of the succeeding immigrants and the indigenous population. Consequently, conflicts in majority-minority relations were perceived as individual differences at the micro level of interaction, and these could be resolved by consensus among the individuals involved.

The same perspective was applied to the immigration experience. Voluntary immigration was perceived as the result of individual decisions and actions. The contacts between the immigrants and the host peoples were principally viewed as the interaction of individuals at the micro level, without considering the macro structures that constrained the interaction at the micro level. The differences between the immigrants and the host society were viewed as mere matters of adjustment and consensus, usually by the former, and assimilation of the immigrants to the majority's idealized social order would be just a matter of time.

There are two general immigration patterns which are applicable to the United States' experience - voluntary and involuntary immigration. At one extreme are the voluntary immigrants, the political, economic and intellectual elite who are free to move about as they please, many of whom maintain their legal citizenship but have residences or domiciles in various parts of the world. Closely following would be officials or employees of international and regional organizations such as the United Nations and multinational corporations. The other extreme, the involuntary immigrants, are exemplified by the original black slaves who were forcibly brought to the American continent. Following them would be the refugees, the result of war, political persecution, economic deprivation or natural disasters.

Between would be the millions of immigrants who have peopled the United States. Some would be those who saw migration as the only way to improve their economic situation or that of their children - the displaced peasants and urban proletariat of Europe and Asia. Since World War II there has been an increasing number who did not find it necessary to immigrate, but rather did so in search of economic and intellectual "greener pastures". They usually came from middle and upper class backgrounds, had higher educational or occupational credentials or professions, and since the 1960s, have also been referred to as the "brain drain".

In a sense, with the exception of the extremes of voluntary and involuntary immigrants, all immigrants are refugees to some degree. Migration requires a heavy commitment to invest in high social, psychological, economic, political and cultural costs. Moreover, it is an action which, once consummated, is difficult, and for most immigrants impossible to reverse. In other words, people who are not totally deprived (real or perceived) and who see a reasonable economic and political future for themselves and their children will not easily take such a significant step. Therefore, most immigrants feel compelled to immigrate.

We therefore posit that, in general, migration is precipitated by macro historical, economic and political factors over which the immigrants have little or no control. The same may be said in regard to the disposition towards and interaction with the immigrants by the host peoples. To wit, the immigration policies and laws of the host countries and the disposition of the host peoples toward the immigrants are influenced by macro historical, economic and political factors over which the latter have little or no control.

Finally, we suggest that immigration is not only a process involving individuals (immigrants and host), but is also an interaction between economic, social and political systems and interaction or clash between cultures.

SCOPE AND DIRECTION OF THE STUDY

It would seem that the interaction of forces emerging from macro and micro levels are critical in understanding the institutional, behavioral and attitudinal factors that operate among immigrants in the new environment. They will be related to their definitions and perceptions of the necessary social action needed to resolve or minimize conflicts and demands which they confront. Thus, this study departs from the traditional description or analysis of a particular group of immigrants' "American experience", or "how they made it in America". Its major focus is on the immigration and integration process itself rather than the people involved. It uses an open-ended approach with an historical perspective. This allows wider parameters with which to examine the issues raised, rather than the limitations of proving or disproving narrowly defined predetermined hypotheses.

The study examines certain aspects of race and ethnic relations in America, using a conflict and change model and multilevel analysis. In general, the

study addresses itself to examining the macro and micro structures that precipitated the "voluntary" immigration of a group of nonwhite immigrants to
the United States. It also examines the manner in which these structures
influenced the immigration process itself, as well as the interaction and
integration of the group with Americans and American institutions.

In addressing the issues raised by this undertaking, the study will examine
the Pilipino (or Filipino-American) immigration experience, rather than the
Pilipinos in the United States. At this juncture, it may be appropos to explain
the use of the term "Pilipino" rather than the common "Filipino" when
referring to the inhabitants or citizens of the Philippines.

The Philippines was named "Las Islas Filipinas" (Philippine Islands) after
Felipe (Philip) II of Spain (1527-1598). During the Spanish colonization of
the country, Spaniards born of Spanish parents in the Philippines were called
"Españoles Filipinos" (Philippine Spaniards) or simply "Filipinos" to distinguish
them from Spaniards born in Spain who were referred to as "Españoles Peninsulares" (Peninsular Spaniards). Persons of mixed native and European
parentage were called "mestizos" and the pure blooded natives as "Indios"
(Indians) (Albella, 1971).

When the United States took over the Philippines from Spain, the name
was Anglicized to "Philippines", although the non-European and non-Chinese
were referred to in the Hispanic, "Filipino" for male and "Filipina" for female.
None of the major Philippine languages has an "f" sound. Therefore, the
people refer to their country as "Republika Ng Pilipinas" (Republic of the
Philippines) or simply "Pilipinas", and themselves as "Pilipinos" (masculine)
or "Pilipinas" (feminine). This study will retain the English "Philippines"
when referring to the country, but will use the native term "Pilipino" when
referring to the people.

The choice of Pilipinos as a case with which to examine the concerns of this
study was dictated by conceptual and practical considerations. First, among
the three major Asian groups in the U.S. (Chinese, Japanese and Pilipinos),
the Pilipinos come from a nation with the longest colonial experience. In fact,
China and Japan were never colonized by any power in the classical sense. The
Philippines was a colony of Spain for approximately three centuries and of the
United States for about half a century. Further, it continued to be a dependency
of the U.S. long after its political independence from the U.S. in 1946.

This experience provides a typical as well as a unique example of the
movement of people from a colony to the colonizing country, during and
after the era of colonialization. As a colony of the U.S., Pilipinos could move
freely to the continental U.S. and U.S territories without the constraints of
immigration laws. Until recently, many former colonial powers (*i.e.,* Britain,
France, the Netherlands, etc.) were rather liberal concerning migration from
their former colonies. Spain has been liberal with the movement of Pilipinos
either as immigrants or otherwise. In fact, nationals of both countries may
have dual citizenship and go into either country without entry visas. However,
this was not the case between the U.S. and the Philippines. As soon as the
Philippines was set on the road to independence in 1935 (as a commonwealth),
immigration of Pilipinos was immediately restricted and subjected to the

national quotas of origin from non-European countries, in spite of the fact that from 1935 to 1946 the Philippines had theoretically the same status as Puerto Rico has today.

The large migrations of Pilipinos to the U.S. which began during the early part of this century became a trickle in 1935, and resumed in large numbers after the promulgation of the U.S. Immigration and Nationality Act of 1965.

The Philippines is not the largest Asian source of immigrants in terms of population and territory. Also, with the exception of Japan, the Philippines' state of development (or underdevelopment) is about the same as that of other countries in the region. Nevertheless, the largest group of immigrants from Asia has been and continues to be from the Philippines. Since U.S immigration laws generally do not favor immigration from the Philippines, this phenomenon, especially the brain drain type migration, suggests more than the individual decisions and actions of immigrants. Thus, this study may not only provide unique information on the issues raised here, but also information that may be useful for other similar comparative studies.

Lastly, the nationality (Pilipino), training and cross-cultural experience of the author provided the practical motive for the selection of the group. Of course, as a Pilipino this work will be influenced by national, ethnic, cultural and even personal biases. However, this author's nationality, professional and personal networks provided access to information and contacts with people in the Philippines, the U.S. and elsewhere which otherwise may not have been possible. Also, being a Pilipino comparative sociologist enabled the author to detect, appreciate, analyze and explain peculiarities and nuances in the Philippine social structure, Pilipino personality and social characteristics which a non-Pilipino or those unfamiliar with the country and the people would have bypassed. Hopefully, these practical advantages, combined with the author's broad cross-cultural perspective and experience, will help neutralize any personal, ethnic or cultural prejudices.

ORGANIZATION OF THE BOOK

This book presents a comprehensive look at the Pilipino immigration experience to the United States of America. In order to understand this experience, it was deemed necessary to include an examination of the historically developed macro structures that precipitated the migration and later integration of Pilipinos to the U.S. These include a closer look at preimmigration information about the Philippines and Pilipinos, as well as the contemporary network of relationships between the Philippines and the U.S. which influence the interaction of the Pilipinos in their new environment at the micro level.

Chapter I provides conceptual and theoretical considerations on the issues of immigration and consequent perceptions of and interaction among immigrants and the host peoples. Chapter II provides information on Pilipinos, the Philippines and its history; examines selected traditional and contemporary aspects of the Philippine social structure and institutions, as well as some aspects of Pilipino personality and social characteristics; and provides information on the contemporary Pilipino population in the U.S., *vis-à-vis* the rest of the U.S. population. Chapter III examines with an historical perspective the internal and external political, economic, social, military and cultural factors in the Philippines and the United States that led to the development of the macro structures precipitating the migration of Pilipinos to the latter. Chapter IV examines how these macro structures determined the periods of Pilipino immigration to the U.S.; the types of immigrants across time; how the same structures influenced the perceptions of the interaction. Chapter V examines and describes what it means to be a Pilipino in the United States, namely a nonwhite immigrant minority, and also examines how the historically developed and current macro structures in both countries influence this. The last chapter summarizes and examines the implications of the study and provides some conceptual and theoretical suggestions in viewing majority and minority relations in general and the immigration process in particular.

THE IMMIGRANT AS PART OF A MACRO AND MICRO SYSTEM AND PROCESS

International immigration, with the exception of mass movements of refugees, is to some extent a process in which the most active agents are the immigrants themselves. However, migration patterns are influenced by and operate within a sociohistorical, economic, political and military institutional framework with international, transnational and regional dimensions. These are variables that could determine the patterns of immigration as an international phenomenon, as well as the movement of one group of people from one country to another *vis-à-vis* other countries. Moreover, these historical, economic, political and military variables on an international level or between the source of immigrants and host country could also influence the manner by which the social-cultural contact between the immigrating and host cultures occur.

The extent to which a more realistic understanding of immigrants and their networks and relationships develop will depend on a more holistic orientation and approach. It is not enough to study the immigrant minorities at their point of entry in the host society, although they are the ultimate actors in the process of immigration. It is also esssential to understand their premigration status and patterns of relationships. On another level, it is important to understand the interaction of institutional and interpersonal factors as these intertwine to affect the nature and characteristics of immigrant communities in America. It is, therefore, proposed that a more accurate conceptual and empirical analysis of immigration include dimensions of macro and micro systemic relationships and processes.

The Macro Level

At the macro level are larger networks and systems of relationships that have been historically conditioned. For instance, major international events such as World Wars I and II and the consequent changes in the international power structure contributed to international and transnational migration patterns. An example would be the change in the destination of Jewish immigrants from the U.S. to the new (1948) state of Israel. Other examples are the massive migration of Cuban and Vietnamese refugees to the U.S. Although the East Europeans (particularly Hungarians), Cubans and Vietnamese were all supposed to be fleeing from Communism, the differential treatment accorded the Vietnamese was notable. Some of the negative reception accorded to the Vietnamese can be attributed to their arrival in the U.S. when the country was experiencing a recession, while some of it must be attributed to racism. However, the resentment against the Vietnamese immigrants may also be because they symbolize the nation that gave the United States its first internationally embarrassing defeat and political debacle.

A critical concern is the political and economic relationship that brings about change and conflict between societies resulting in the domination of a nation or region by other nations or power alliances. One such structural relationship that has had a direct bearing on immigration is colonialism. Under that system, initial immigration was usually from the colonial country to the colonized territories. Although the immigrant-colonizers may have belonged to various social classes of the mother country, they assumed superordinate positions over the colonized peoples. One pattern was to rule a territory indirectly through the native elite, many of whom were "educated" by the colonial administrators (some in the mother country), thereby making them more effective brokers between the colonizers and the rest of the population. Paradoxically, some of the native elite educated by their colonial masters, having absorbed liberal, progressive and socialist ideas in Europe, became the leaders of the nationalist movements and revolutions that eventually severed the colonial ties.

However, regardless of their social and political positions in their own country and in spite of their education, the native elite continued to have a status subordinate to that of the colonizers whether they were in Europe, in the colonizer's country or in their own. In other words, by the structural subordinate relationships of the colonized natives, regardless of any superior personal attributes that they may have had, they were still perceived and treated as inferiors by the colonizer. Indeed, in addition to economic advantages, an attribute of colonialism and structural racism was the privilege that even the lowest white man (colonizer) had over the highest colonized native elite (Fanon, 1968; Prager, 1972-73:117-150).

The end of the colonial era brought a change in migration patterns between the colonized and colonizers. Except for the U.S., Canada and Australia, it is now the former colonized peoples who immigrate to their former mother countries. Nevertheless, most of the immigrants from the former colonies still maintain an inferior status in their new countries, in spite of the fact that "independence" is supposed to have given equal status with former colonial masters (Hunt and Walker, 1974:298-327). This is partly due to the fact that the independence achieved by decolonization was replaced by neocolonialism, whereby the emphasis was on continued economic dominance, albeit in more subtle forms. Whereas colonialism was maintained by military fiat, neocolonialism is maintained by treaties and by bilateral or regional agreements between the developed (former colonizers) and underdeveloped (former colonies) countries.

The status of dependency in neocolonialism is often maintained by multinational corporations. Although these corporations often enjoy the protection of the former colonial governments, their goal is the accumulation of profits without regard for the interest of the Third World countries as well as their own. While they may provide capital investments and some employment, the fact is that by the very nature of their capitalist corporate structure they take more from Third World countries than they put in. Additionally, they extract and deplete natural resources, along with cheap labor, of Third World countries and often cause irreparable damage to the environment and ecology (Jalee, 1968; Edwards, *et. al.,* 1972:409-457).

Colonial rule, even with the collaboration of elements of the native elite, had to be maintained by naked force since it was resisted by the majority of the colonized peoples. The domination of multinationals is more subtle, as it gives the appearance of providing benefits and, therefore, is accepted and even desired by the people adversely affected by it. In the short run, a large corporate operation in a Third World region, besides providing employment, develops infrastructures (ports, roads, airports) and provides government revenues which otherwise would have to be raised through taxes. In the long run, the multinationals do not benefit the host countries. More often than not their operations are aimed at world markets and are irrelevant to the needs of developing countries. The operations would benefit the host countries more if they were owned and operated by natives (Barnet, 1974).

The structural networks of inequality between nations and regions, which are brought about by colonialism, neocolonialism or international and national events such as wars and revolutions, have a direct effect on national structures. For instance, they retard the development of Third World nations into economically and politically viable nation states. In effect, they create and perpetuate the structural factors that precipitate emigration. Structurally, they lead to the creation of an international pool of reserve labor, ready and willing to go wherever and whenever they are needed.

If potential immigrants have little or no control over the factors that precipitate their emigration from their countries of origin, they may have even less control over the structural factors that precipitate or constrain their immigration to other countries. These structures are also historically conditioned by events and manipulated by the networks, countries or regions that gain the most from international immigration. They are the international, regional and bilateral agreements between countries as well as unilateral immigration laws that determine the movement of people from one country to another.

One example would be the advent and expansion of international and regional organizations: the United Nations and its agencies, North Atlantic Treaty Organization (NATO); European Common Market (EC); Association of Southeast Asian Nations (ASEAN); and the "multinationals". These networks have created bureaucracies wherein people of divergent origins, races and orientations are able to work and live together in a crosscultural atmosphere. Unlike the traditional immigrants who may change their nationalities, these people have become the international bureaucrats or technocrats, or, as in the case of those connected with the EC, the "Eurocrats" (Lerner, 1969).

Their immediate and primary concerns and perhaps loyalties are with the organizations to which they are connected, be it an intergovernmental organization or a multinational, rather than any one nation. Many are not even immigrants in the normal definition of the term, but move from one part of the world to another and are transient residents of any country where the organization sends them. For most, their only national identity is their passport. Since their interpersonal relationships are based on professional networks rather than on ethnicity, religion or politics, the individual or societal effects of these relations on their social and cultural perspectives may take on a different dimension. They may in fact belong to what Useem, Useem and Donoghue (1963:169-179; 167:130-1143) call the "third culture", *i.e.,* people who straddle two or more cultures and sometimes find themselves uncomfortable in any one culture.

It can be and has been argued that persons connected with developmental type organizations such as the United Nations and other agencies (World Bank, etc.) do contribute to regional development as well as to individual countries, and additionally give prestige to their countries of origin. It is doubtful, however, if people connected with the multinationals will be concerned for their own country's development over their organization's profitability. Aside from absorbing some of the skilled manpower needed by a country, there is the possibility that the persons hired by the multinationals often become the agents by which these corporations prevent the development of native enterprises or national movements that would reduce the margins of profits of the foreign corporations in Third World countries (Adams, 1968; Bello, *et al.,* 1969:93-146; Baran and Sweezey, 1972:435-442; Weisskopf, 1972:443-457; Pomeroy, 1974).

Another example of structural factors controlling immigration would be the immigration laws of individual countries as well as regional arrangements on the international movement of nationals, such as the relative freedom of people between the countries belonging to the EC, or those belonging to the British Commonwealth of Nations, which has recently been unilaterally restricted by Britain.

Still another example is that, although the U.S. was always a desired place to which to immigrate by Third World peoples, they were prevented from doing so by U.S. immigration laws which limited the number of non-whites that could be admitted to the country as immigrants. On the other hand, because of former colonial ties, most Third World immigrants could easily immigrate to their former European mother countries, which had more liberal immigration laws for former colonials.

U.S. legal-political structures that control the entry of immigrants to the U.S. have been and still are dictated by economic and political development of the country, with some sprinkling of concern for the "poor, the sick and the tired". This is evident by the inconsistencies of the immigration laws controlling the entry of nonwhite immigrants.

Nevertheless, the U.S. continues to be attractive to peoples of all races from all over the world. In spite of the economic difficulties the U.S. has gone through, it is still preferred over the situations that precipitate emigration. Barriers to economic advancement in the immigrant's own country are institutionalized and actually experienced, in contrast with the popular image of America as the land of equal opportunities.

Racism in America may have been discussed in academic, intellectual and political circles and in the urban media. However, except perhaps in social-ist/communist countries or in those regions with strong anti-American political ideologies, the racial issues in the U.S. hardly filter through to the rest of the population, if at all. Consequently, in spite of their experience with institutional racism or social discrimination in their own countries, potential immigrants from Third World regions still perceive the racial issue in the U.S, as being caused by racist or prejudiced persons who are "sick" or illiterate. Their sources of information, the popular media and *Gone with the Wind* type movies, whether imported or the local versions, still depict the social-psychological pathology model of racism. This is evidenced by long waiting lists of visa applicants and the backlog in processing visas by the U.S. Immigration and Naturalization Service. An ocular examination of any U.S. Consulate where there are no controls on emigration will show lines of people waiting just to get the appropriate immigration application forms.

Because the U.S. is the only major protagonist in the two World Wars that did not suffer defeat or physical destruction, and with the advent of the bipolarization of the world between the Communist countries and the "free", in which the U.S. is perceived as the leader of the latter and the most likely noncommunist nation to survive in a shooting war with communists, the U.S. has become even more attractive to most peoples of the world seeking a new and better life.

Another dimension to be considered is the various changes in the political, economic and social atmosphere in the U.S. at the time of immigration. Wilhelm (1970) recorded how discrimination against blacks relaxed and then turned vicious at various points in U.S. history, depending on whether they were needed by the economy or not. McWilliams (1964) also reports the same inconsistent attitudes and behavior against the immigrant minorities, such as the Chinese, Japanese, Pilipinos and Mexicans (in addition to blacks, Hispanics, Native Americans and even poor whites). Not only were attitudes and behavior inconsistent, but so were U.S. immigration policies, laws and practices. These were liberalized when these immigrants were needed and restricted when they were not. This is not to deny the U.S. or any country the right of promulgating immigration policies motivated by national interest. However, the National Commission on Manpower Policy (NCMP) contends that the U.S. is the only major country hosting immigrants that did not and still does not have a consistent immigration policy. What it has had are policies and laws that change according to the dictates of domestic and international circumstances (NCMP, 1978).

The relationships between the U.S. and the countries of origin of the immigrants, whether bilateral or part of an international network, also affect the immigration process. The previous ties between immigrants from a former colony to a former colonizer country has already been noted. Another instance would be that, if the position of a small nonwhite country with no previous ties to the U.S. was crucial to the latter's interest in the East-West confrontation, more likely than not official attitudes and treatment of immigrants would be favorable. The U.S. government might even take steps to reduce or eliminate any discrimination immigrants from this particular country would encounter - perhaps even more than they would for minority American citizens.

The attitudes and behavior of the population toward immigrants are also influenced to some extent by these relationships, whether they are in concert or different from those of the government. The best known examples are the treatment accorded German immigrants or Americans of German descent during World War I and the Japanese during World War II - which culminated in the incarceration of the latter for the duration of the war (Yin, 1973:131; Kitano, 1874:79). One notes the differential treatment given to refugees from Haiti, a country that is allegedly anticommunist, *vis-à-vis* the refugees from Cuba, a communist country - although the "welcome mat" for the Cuban refugees seems to have worn out. The differential treatment may have some racist overtones - the Haitians are black while the Cubans are mainly white. One wonders if political refugees from South Korea or the Philippines (anti-communist countries and allies of the U.S.) would be given the same treatment as the refugees from Indochina (the "boat people").

To reiterate, historically-developed marcoeconomic, political and social structures, over which the immigrants have little or no control, do have influence both before and following the immigration process.

The macro structures creating the push and pull factors that determine immigration invariably impinge on internal national structures and ultimately the societal network of the individuals affected. Thus, societal and psychological conflicts with the environment that heretofore may have been resolved internally are now perceived as soluble only by immigration to a new (and alien) society.

The Micro Dimension

At the micro level are those individual goals, aspirations and societal value systems that may have precipitated migration. They include significant sources of conflict at the personal or familial level which may be resolved by migrating; for instance, individual professional or intellectual aspirations which may be constrained by political, social, economic and value systems in the home country. There may also be conflict between acquired "Western" or "modern" values and traditional values and norms. Moreover, they influence the immigrants' perceptions and patterns of contact and interactions in the host society.

Another factor at the micro level that should be considered are the different preimmigration backgrounds of immigrants from the same country across time and contemporaneously. Immigrants at the end of the 19th and early 20th centuries would come from similar social and economic backgrounds, occupations, the same village or even be related to each other. This pattern has been changing since the end of World War II, as shown by reports from the Immigration and Naturalization Service (INS). Although excluded in our definition of voluntary immigrants, the Vietnamese refugees' backgrounds range from unschooled peasants to economic, political, intellectual and social elites. If these Vietnamese "immigrants" did not relate to each other in Vietnam, it is unlikely that they will in the U.S., other than sharing an ethnic/racial heritage and common war experience. The same may be said with the early unschooled, rural origins of the first Pilipino immigrants and the more recent Pilipino immigrants from middle to upper class social/economic backgrounds with high educational and occupational credentials.

The average Americans (or any host people) do not make these differentiations of immigrants from the same country. Cubans are Cubans, Poles are Poles, Vietnamese are Vietnamese - or worse, white and nonwhite immigrants are lumped into general categories. Attitudes towards immigrants from a particular country are guided by stereotypes gained by direct experience or secondhand knowledge. The few that do not fit into the stereotype become the "exceptions".

The "Brain Drain"

Another more recent critical issue which relates to broader consequences of immigration for the larger international system and of particular importance for both the host and country of origin is the "brain drain". Broadly defined, the brain drain refers to persons of high qualifications and skills of one country being employed elsewhere. Another narrower "economic" definition of the phenomenon refers to those persons whose education and training have been made possible through the efforts of one country, but whose services are utilized by another (Bello *et al.,* 1969:93-146). The brain drain illustrates: 1) the manner by which external structures affect the individual's decision and ability to immigrate; and 2) how the macro network changes over time and dictates the type and nature of the immigrants.

Until the promulgation of the U.S. 1965 Immigration and Nationality Act, the brain drain was mostly a European problem, especially of the former European colonies. For instance, one of the major political issues in Britain in the 1960s was the emigration of the highly educated from Britain to North America, Australia, New Zealand and even Africa.[1] At the same time, Britain was making full use of doctors from its former colonies (particularly Indian and Pakistan) who were willing to work for less than British doctors would in National Health Service areas. What is more significant was the net effect the

[1] Paradoxically, large numbers of British-born as well as African-born English-speaking Rhodesians are migrating back to Britain since the inception of majority black rule. It is most likely that many South Africans, particularly those with English ancestry, may also do the same in the future.

brain drain had on the source countries, which was not precipitated but merely accelerated by the new U.S. immigration law. This means that developing countries were and are losing the type of people they need most for their development, and those who are left (and are barred from migrating elsewhere because of their low educational or occupational credentials) are those who can hardly help themselves, much less their country's development. The net effect of the international migration of the talented and skilled is an additional loss to the countries of origin and gain for the developed countries and the international organizations that engage their services.

The Immigration and Nationality Act of 1965 changed the pattern of immigration to the United States, particularly as it affected Third World countries. This immigration law increased the quotas of fifty to a hundred persons a year for nonwhite nations to 20,000 per year setting umbrella quotas for the Eastern and Western Hemispheres. While this radically increased the number of persons that could immigrate from Third World (*i.e.,* nonwhite) countries, the law tends to be selective towards those with high educational or occupational qualifications. In less than a decade after the promulgation of the Act, the majority of immigrants to the U.S. were coming from Third World nations, replacing Europe as the major source of immigrants. Moreover, they were no longer the "poor and the tired" and unskilled, but the better educated from the higher social classes in their own societies (Keely, 1971: 157-169). They were more typical of the post World War II international brain drain migrants.

The brain drain problem suggests that the study of immigrants not only has important conceptual and research implications, but also relates to questions of national and international policies. At the micro level are the new immigrants, different from those before World War II. The higher their qualifications, the wider are those professional and personal networks which may transcend ethnic and/or national boundaries. Their perceptions of the universe are wider and deeper, and they are in a better position to sell their labor (talents) in a competitive market. Conceptually, race, ethnicity and/or traditional social structures, values and norms become less important in establishing social relationships.

At the macro level, containing the brain drain becomes the burden of the countries negatively affected by it. Their economic, political and military dependence on the developed nations and multinationals prevents them from creating the economic, political and intellectual climate that would restrain emigrants from leaving, without an outright curtailment of an individual's freedom to travel. Most countries do not resort to this, and the few that do are severely criticized. Most countries tolerate the brain drain with the hope that it will somehow contribute to development; that it will decrease the problem of unemployment among the educated who are more "dangerous" than the uneducated; and that remittances of dollars earned abroad will contribute to the country's balance of payments. In the long run these are untenable aspirations, for the dollars the brain drain remits do not compensate for the investments made in the emigrants' education. The contribution to their country's development had they stayed would have been more significant than the money remitted (Weisskopf, 1872:442-475).

SUMMARY

In summary, it is suggested that studies in majority-minority relations which focus on immigrant ethnic groups should be extended conceptually. The traditional approach of focusing on the individual immigrants as the sole and principal actors in the process of immigration should be modified. Analysis should include examination of conflicts that may be generated at various levels and how these change temporarily and spatially, before the immigrants leave their country of origin and after they arrive in the new environment. Furthermore, understanding of the process of the immigrants' attempts to adjust to a new culture should expand beyond the interpersonal relationships of the immigrants and the host people. They should include a closer look at the larger structural networks across time and space that determine or constrain the types of personal interactions in majority-minority relations involving immigrants and host population.

Therefore, this study takes the position that the extent to which immigrants are faced with competing demands, conflicts and constraints in American society may be a consequence of their individual status, intragroup, intergroup and cross-cultural perceptions, experiences and relationships. These competing demands, conflicts and constraints may have their genesis in the country of origin, in the host country or in an international network of relationships over which the immigrants and the hosts had little or no control.

Using past and current immigration from the Philippines to the United States, this study examines the historical, economic, political, social, military and cultural macro and micro structures in the immigrants' country of origin and destination and the world across time and space, which may have precipitated their immigration and affected their patterns of adjusting and surviving in their new environment.

2. *Who are the Pilipinos?*

Prior to the latter part of the nineteenth century, few Americans had even heard of the Philippines or Pilipinos. The acquisition of the Philippines by the United States from Spain and its subsequent colonialization generated a controversy in the American body politic that has only since been equalled by the controversy generated by the Vietnam War. The Philippines and the Pilipinos were again brought to the American public's attention during the Depression of the 1930s and the height of the controversy surrounding the attempts to exclude Pilipino migrant labor from the U.S. World War II brought attention to the Philippines as allies of the U.S. against Japan, which was dramatized by the battles for Bataan and Corregidor and, of course, General Douglas MacArthur's "I shall return" after he was driven from the country by the Japanese (Wolfe, 1961; Miller, 1982).

In the mid 1970s, the Philippines was brought to U.S. and international attention when President Ferdinand E. Marcos, before the end of his second and last term of office according to the 1935 constitution, declared martial law, suspending the constitution and civil liberties. Not withstanding a subsequent promulgation of a new constitution, elections of a new assembly and "lifting" of martial law, he continues to rule the country by Presidential Decrees. The Philippines was again brought national and international attention by the assassination of former Senator Benigo S. Aquino, Jr., a popular opposition leader, on August 21, 1983, at the Manila International Airport upon his arrival after three years of self-exile in the U.S. Since then, news about the Philippines and the Marcos regime has been frequently in the U.S and international media, in the same manner as the last years of the Shah of Iran or the Samoza regimes were.

Since America's first contact with the Philippines and Pilipinos, there have been a number of scholarly studies and publications about the country. Among the most significant was Blair and Robertson's multivolume, *The*

Philippine Islands, published in 1903. More relevant to the concerns of this book was Bruno Lasker's, *Filipino Immigration to Continental United States and Hawaii,* originally published in 1931; and Carey McWilliam's *Factories in the Fields* (1939) and *Brothers Under the Skin* (1964). There are also a number of dissertations, theses and articles in learned or professional journals.[2] Professor Emory S. Bogardus of the University of Southern California was among the first American scholars interested in Pilipinos in the U.S., and became one of the defenders of Pilipino rights and interests. He authored several reports and articles, most of which were published in *Sociology and Social Research.* Three other works should be mentioned. They are: *America Is in the Heart* by Carlos Bulusan (1946);[3] *I Lived with Americans* by Manuel Buaken (1948): and *Makibaka - The Pilipino American Struggle* by Royal F. Morales (1974). The latter is a reexamination and critique of the assimilationist model as viewed by the experience of Pilipinos for more than half a century. The works of Bulusan and Buaken reflect personal accounts and common experiences. What makes the two interesting are the differences in their preimmigration backgrounds. Carlos Bulusan came from a rural background and the lowest economic class, while Manuel Buaken came from professional, middle class and cosmopolitan parentage.

However, from this study's perspective the works by Lasker and McWilliam are the most relevant and informative. Lasker's book was the first comprehensive work on Pilipino immigration to the U.S., which included analysis of the preimmigration network and characteristics of the Pilipino immigrants. Both of McWilliam's works dealt with immigrant and nonimmigrant minority groups, among which were the Pilipinos. They provide a good understanding of the macro economic and political structures that determined the manner by which the Pilipinos and others fared in the American system.

Most of the information the American public receives concerning Pilipinos is from the popular media and political rhetoric rather than from the books mentioned. The political rhetoric comes from well known political figures such as Henry Cabot Lodge, Sr. and Theodore Roosevelt, who were against Pilipino interests, as well as those who stood for Philippine and Pilipino interests such as Andrew Carnegie and Mark Twain. Nonetheless, most of the media information ranges from half truths to falsehoods, from the idyllic to the bizarre.

It is, therefore, apropos that since this work is about the Pilipinos in America, some aspects about the Philippines and the Pilipinos be examined for a better appreciation of their experience in the United States. The information presented may not be unique to the Philippines, but the social

[2]Lasker's work, which was orginally published by the University of Chicago Press in 1931, has been reprinted by the Arno Press Inc., and the New York Times in 1969; McWilliam's *Brothers Under the Skin* was originally published in 1942. Another comprehensive work on the early Pilipino immigrants is a doctoral dissertation by Benecio T. Catapusan, "Social Adjustment of Filipinos in the United States". University of California, 1940. It has been published by R and E Associates, San Francisco, California, 1972.

[3] *America Is the Heart* was originally published by Harcourt, Brace and Company in 1942, and was reprinted by the University of Washington Press, Seattle in 1973.

structures, institutions, values and norms presented, like those of all people, are not static in the push towards the twenty-first century. A brief examination of current data on Pilipinos in the United States comes mainly from the 1970 U.S. Census of Population.

THE PHILIPPINES: LAND AND PEOPLE

The Philippines is composed of 7,000 islands and islets of which about 800 are inhabited. From its northernmost islands of Batanes one can see across the North China Sea to the contours of the outlying islands of Taiwan, and its southernmost islands (the Tawi-tawi group and Palawan) are only a few hours by boat to Kota Kinabalu in Sabah, Malaysia. Its closest neighbor to the west across the South China Sea is Indochina and to the east across the Pacific Ocean is the U.S. island of Guam. There are three major island groups. The largest is Luzon to the north; the second largest is Mindanao to the south; and in between are the smaller island groups called the Visayas. The Philippines has a land area of 114,830 square miles and the whole archipelago is crisscrossed with rivers, streams and mountain ranges of volcanic origin, some of which continue to be active. It has a tropical climate and its average temperature throughout the year is 70 degrees Fahrenheit.

Most of the land is fertile and the tropical climate permits year-round cultivation. Its seas and fresh water bodies provide most of the people's food. Every school child in the country is told that the Philippines is endowed with rich natural resources and climate so that it can support twice its present population of a little over 40 million. The Spaniards, upon their arrival, called it "Las Islas del Poniente" (Island of the Western Breeze). The Pilipino scholar and national hero, Jose Rizal, in his poem "My Last Farewell" written the night preceding his execution by Spanish authorities, called it "La Perla del Oriente" - the Pearl of the Orient-Sea.

From an airplane, one can see the patterns of human settlement along the sea coast, river deltas, the plateaus of Mindanao, the plains of Central Luzon and the Island of Panay. There is some geological evidence that the Philippines was once connected to the mainland of Asia through land bridges which disappeared at the coming of the Ice Age. What seems to be a stronger evidence of the land bridge theory is the existence of a group of people that are racially identical with the Pygmies of Africa. They are, in fact, the oldest known inhabitants of the archipelago. The Spaniards called them *Negritos* "little Negroes" and the name has since stuck among the educated Pilipino, although they are also called *Ate, Ayta* and *Dumagats* (Rahman, 1963:137-157).

Like most tribal or "primitive" people, the Negritos and other tribal minorities are now in a numerical minority through genocide and disease. They have been driven from their ancestral lands and fishing grounds by "advancing civilization" and, in general, have suffered the same fate as the original natives of the American continent. However, since the late 1960s, the government has given them protection, including restoration of some of their lands, and granted them reservations where they will not be disturbed, but where they can have access to health facilities and educational opportunities

(PANAMIN, 1970; MacLeish and Conger, 1972:220-225).[4]

The majority of the population is basically of Malay stock with some intermingling of foreign blood such as Chinese, Spanish, American and Indian. The Malays supposedly came from what is now Malaysia and Indonesia, and migrated to the islands in large numbers some 7,000 years ago (Sawyer, 1900; Krober, 1928; Landa-Jocano, 1965:56-78). The present Pilipinos belong to eight major ethnolinguistic groups, made up of 200 dialects (Fox and Flory, 1974). The eight major groups are: Tagalog, Ilocano, Pampango, Pangasinan and Bicolano in Luzon; and Warray Hiligaynor and Sugboanon in the Visayan islands. The Muslims on the Island of Mindanao have their own language and culture, and to these were added the major languages from the rest of the islands as a result of internal migration. Those of mixed blood are known as *mestizos.* If they have a foreign heritage other than Spanish, they are identified by that, *e.g.,* those with Chinese blood are Chinese mestizos, etc. The term mestizo by itself connotes Spanish heritage, which implies some social status during the Spanish colonial era.

Pilipinos also have their own notions of racial superiority as this applies to their brownish complexion. A legend that almost every child is taught dwells on how God (*Bathala*) created the first human being. The legend also reflects the ancient art and technology of pottery. God fashioned the first human being to his image from clay and placed it in the kiln to be fired. He let it stay too long and the image was burnt black, and thus was the first black person created. At the second attempt, God was too cautious and did not get the right temperature and firing time. The image was "uncooked" and too pale, and became the first white person. In his third attempt, Bathala had the right mixture of clay and had the kiln temperature and firing time just right. The result was the creation of the first man that was truly in the image of God, the brown man.

There are some covert differences among the major groups in terms of food, customs, traditions and modes of dress, but the major discriminating differences are in the languages and ways they identify themselves. If a person spoke Tagalog and identified him/herself as Tagalog, then he/she is accepted as Tagalog. There is a strong regional linguistic consciousness. When Pilipinos meet, the first thing they do is identify themselves by their regional or language affinities. Many of the gesselschaft-type organizations in urban centers are based on regional and language origins. Just as American students often segregate themselves by race, the Pilipinos do so by language group or regional origins.

However, aside from language, any major distinctions in race and cultural traits disappear. Fox (1961:6-9; 1963:342-346) contends that the distinction is geoeconomic rather than linguocultural. There is a difference in lifestyles between those who live on the coast and make their living in fishing and commerce and those who live in the interior and make their living on the

---

[4] These "reservations" should not be equated with those of the American Indians. In the Philippines, "tribal" minorities declared their own ancestral lands (or what was left of it) as reservations. This land is usually exempt from torrence title laws and is off limits to settling and development by "outsiders".

land. Corpus (1965:2-13) uses a rural-urban dichotomy, associating cultural traits with major economic activity. About forty percent of the population live in urban areas; they are educated and make their living through a money market system. About 60 percent live in rural areas and make their living on the land, some of whom are still in the barter economy. Thus there is a dual economic system and culture.

Pre-Western (Spanish) cultural influences came from China, Japan, India, Indochina and Arabia. The religion and nation of Islam were the dominant religious and cultural influences prior to the coming of the Spaniards. However, through political and military actions, Spanish colonization aborted the spread of the religion beyond the island of Mindanao. Today, the Muslims comprise about 4 percent of the population. Among all the Pilipino groups they are the only ones who have resisted any foreign cultural or political inclusion or domination during the close to four centuries of colonization by Spain and the U.S.; they continue to do so against the present government. The Philippine Constitution and various laws were passed to recognize their distinctiveness from the rest of the population, but their continued insistence on economic, cultural and political autonomy, which includes skirmishes with the military, constitute the "Muslim problem" in the nation (Majul, 1973).

Over 80 percent of the population are Christians, of whom approximately 10 percent are of various Protestant sects and the rest are Roman Catholics. Most of the literature on the Philippines, be it a grade school text, encyclopedia or tourist brochure, describes the Philippines as the only Christian nation in the Orient and the Pilipinos as the most "Westernized" people in Asia. Scholarly as well as popular discussions on the racial and cultural composition of the Pilipinos depend on which side of the nationalist/traditionalist or "modern" spectrum one is. One contention is that the Pilipinos and Pilipino culture have been Westernized. Another view is that foreign, particularly Western, cultural and institutional incursions have instead been "Filipinized" to fit existing social structures, values and norms. However, there is almost a universal agreement that there is no longer such a thing as pure native Pilipino culture.

Contours of the Philippine Social Structure

The basic unit of Philippine society is the nuclear family. From the nuclear family, it extends to a larger group through affinity and consanguinity and through other networks to an extended family system and larger group. The latter includes alliances of families (Fox, 1961:6-9). Around the family and the extended group evolves Philippine social and individual life. It demands an almost absolute loyalty and allegiance throughout a person's lifetime, so much so that it is almost possible to predict deviant individual behavior. Conflicts of interests between the individual and the family or group are almost always resolved in favor of the latter. The family or group offers material and emotional support and the individual expects it as a matter of right. This partially explains the existence of very few orphanages and homes for the aged, in spite of the existence of poverty among large portions of the population.

The family extends bilaterally through marriage, for marriage is not only the union of two individuals but an alliance of families or groups. A family does not "lose" a son or daughter in a marriage, but rather it gains a son or daughter plus, of course, an alliance with another group. Prearranged nuptials are very rare, but young men and women are consciously or subconsciously aware of the boundaries within which to seek marriage partners. The family does not make absolute demands nor narrow the choices, but if the couple expects the support of both families after the marriage, they must marry those whom both families can at least tolerate, if not actually like.

Potential and real marital problems involve a more complex intergroup conflict, affecting not only the spouses concerned but the alliance as well. The societal value on the viability of marriage and the family is reflected in the society's legal structures by the absence of a divorce law. Until 1972, when Congress was dissolved, the few attempts at enacting some form of a divorce law never succeeded.

This does not mean that marriages never break up. Marital problems that would end in divorce elsewhere are resolved in various ways: church annulments - a complicated, prolonged and expensive process; "legal separation" - a court sanctioned separation from "bed and board", but still prohibiting either partner from marrying while the other is alive; and by mutual consent of all parties concerned. The last one is often preferred, since all parties are spared the unpleasant publicity of annulments and legal separations. Divorces obtained outside the Philippines dissolving marriages contracted in the country are not recognized.[5]

Pre- and Post-Colonial Structure

Many of the aspects of precolonial Philippine social structures are still in existence, albeit manifested differently and somewhat changed. As noted, the basic structure was the nuclear and extended family. Unions or confederations of families and groups formed a larger unit known as the *barangay* - the social, economic, political and military unit of precolonial Philippine society.[6]

Thus, it was and still is that from the nuclear to the extended family and to the barangay, socialization was oriented towards cooperation and communal welfare, rather than towards individualism and individual competition or achievements within the boundaries of the family and the barangay. Individual efforts and achievements are not discouraged but rather are to be shared with the group, just as the group is expected to rally behind the individual in times of need (Fox, 1961:6-9; Landa-Jocano, 1972:59-79).

[5] The illegality of divorces obtained outside the Philippines dissolving marriages contracted in the Philippines has been reiterated by the Philippine Secretary of Justice and the Philippine Consul General in Los Angeles (*Balitaan*, July 1974:7).

[6] Pronounced "bar-run-gay", the term is also applied to the large boats on which families immigrated from the Malay archipelago.

The precolonial barangay was a stratified society composed of the nobles, warriors, freemen and slaves.[7] The power relationships between the classes were paternalistic. Conflicts were with other barangays and not between the classes within the barangays. Spain, and later the U.S., ruled the country through the local established elite. The former also introduced plantation type agriculture, where a few Spanish and native elites had control of the country's wealth. Until recently, this stratification, minus the slaves which the Spaniards abolished, continued to exist. Although much of the basis of power and wealth has since shifted from the land to industry, real estate and business, it is still very much in the hands of the same few families. During the last fifty years there has been an emergence of a middle class composed of those from the professions, trade, and private and government bureaucracies.

Like the precolonial barangays, power is based on factions or alliances of factions (barangays) that cut vertically across the social classes. Once in a position of power, the faction will use the barangay to its advantage to maintain and expand that position. Maintenance of power is dependent upon the support of the masses who traditionally identify with the elites of their own barangay rather than those of the same lower classes, a structure that resembles the traditional feudal system. Although the elite tend to exhibit paternalistic concern towards those who serve them, they have not been adverse to using their power to destroy perceived or real disloyalty.

Those in the lower classes believe that it is to their interest to identify and ally themselves with those in power in their barangay, rather than with those who are similarly situated but who may belong to a different group (barangay). In empirical situations, this means that one's chances of survival and getting ahead in society are better if one is allied and identified with those in power, rather than being an "independent nobody".

The Pilipino does not compete as an individual and individual interests are often superceded by group interests. Rather, Pilipinos compete with and between groups. The conflict and competition for status and power among groups, which sometimes results in violence and tragedy, is as continuous as life itself and is carried in all aspects of Philippine interpersonal and social life (Hollnstiener, 1963). In addition to intermarriage between groups, among the most often used mechanisms to acquire, expand and maintain the group alliances are the highly valued norms of reciprocity and the *compadrazco* system.

Reciprocity or *utang na loob* is a very highly valued social norm. It is a social debt incurred for materials or services received from another, regardless of whether the extrinsic value of the original goods or services is returned or repaid. "Payment" is not always explicitly demanded, but it is expected, though not always in the same value or manner by which a "debt" is incurred.

---

[7] The use of the term slaves to identify those of the lowest social class in pre-colonial Philippine society has since been challenged by scholars. It was the Spaniards who called them slaves. Agoncillo and Alfonso (1967:41-42) called them "dependents" similarly situated as the serfs in feudal Europe. Phelan (1959:20) likewise contends that they were more identical with debt peonage and sharecropping than with the accepted concept of chattel slavery.

Nor are the reciprocal obligations confined to the two original contracting parties. For instance, collection or payment of the debt is expected or demanded in terms of support in an interfactional conflict, even if the original debt was in a form or manner entirely different from the payment expected. Payment of these debts does not eliminate the contractual obligations; it only transfers the same obligation to the most recent beneficiary of the goods or services. Thus the reciprocal obligations are maintained almost indefinitely (Kaut, 1961:256-272; Hollnstiener, 1970:22-49).

Another important social mechanism by which kinship or alliances are expanded is through the *compadrazco* system or what Fox and Lynch call "Ritual Co-Parenthood". The term *compadre* or *comadre* is derived from the Spanish *padre* and *madre,* meaning father and mother. When the Spaniards introduced Catholicism in the Philippines, among the rituals introduced was the requirement of godparents in baptism and confirmations. This merely added to or christianized the Pilipino's propensity to acquire new or expanded kinship groups and alliances. In addition to baptisms and confirmations, the Pilipinos have made godparents or sponsors part of almost any quasi-religious ceremonies such as ordinations, weddings, house blessings and so on. If the Church would allow multiple baptisms and confirmations, the Pilipinos would gladly have children baptized or confirmed several times in their lives in order to expand their alliances.

By Church law and tradition, the requirement of godparents are not just rituals. With it are established contractual obligations between the godparents and the godchild. Principally, the godparent has the obligations to assume the child's moral education should the real parents fail to do so. But as adopted and used by Pilipinos, these obligations are more than just education or moral upbringing. Moreover, they also extend to obligations between the co-parents (child's real parents and godparents). Both families are, therefore, allied through this ritual. Although the godparents normally are the ones obligated to help the godchild, the reverse is also true. The contractual obligations are multidirectional. They are based on who needs the help and who can give it within the boundaries of the alliances incurred under this mechanism (Fox and Lynch, 1956:424-430).

Ethnicity and Social Status

During the Spanish rule and for a few decades thereafter, the mestizos occupied positions of power and economic advantage over the rest of the population. Early reports of the Philippine social stratification system also contend that among the eight ethnolinguistic groups, the Tagalogs had higher economic status and monopolized positions in the bureaucracy in the public and private sectors (Sawyer, 1900; Kroeber, 1928).

In addition to ruling the country through the existing political structure, the Spaniards instituted a stratification system based on race. At the top were the *Espanoles Peninsulares* (Spaniards born in Spain); below them were the *Espanoles Filipinos* (Spaniards born in the Philippines). They were followed by the mestizos (half Pilipino-Spanish), who were folowed by the *quarterones* (one-fourth Spanish blood) and so on down to *Indio puro* (pure Indian). Access to economic opportunities, education and prestige depended on where one was in the complex stratification which cut across the native social structure. Thus a traditional chief or a person of the noble class may have had lower status than one who was not, but who had some Spanish blood, even if he were a bastard. In fact, the term "Filipino" was not used to refer to Pilipinos until the end of the Spanish rule when it was used by the Pilipinos themselves (Corpus, 1965:33-34; 69; Agoncillo and Alfonso, 1967:4-6; 133-34; 150-151; Abella, 1971).[8]

The pre- and post-colonial stratification system and power relationships were not based on the superiority of any of the major ethnic groups over the others. The apparent monopoly of the Tagalogs and some other groups in positions of power, particularly after the colonial era, was by historical accident. It was brought about by the Spaniards' choice of where to locate their administrative and political capital for their Pacific colony. The Spaniards chose Manila, which was in the Tagalog-speaking region. Manila became the administrative, political, economic and cultural center, in short, the metropolis of the region. Thus, from colonial times to the present, anyone who wanted anything, from a good education to access to commercial opportunities and occupational advancement, had to go to Manila, regardless of whether one was a Tagalog or not. Being in Manila meant being a little bit more sophisticated and better informed than those who were in the countryside regardless of one's education or socioeconomic status. Pilipino political leaders, economists, scholars and business leaders came from all over the country, but all either went to school in, or had some exposure to, the cosmopolitan environment of Manila. It was and is not unusual for the provincial rich or politicians who want to be in the national and international network to have residences in the Manila area, in addition to the ones they have or had in their own provinces.

Being exposed to or part of the urbanization process which was going on in Manila, rather than being a Tagalog, became important for individual or organizational upward mobility. Since Manila was geographically located in the Tagalog-speaking region, more Tagalogs were exposed to the process than those who were far from Manila. In fact, Tagalogs who were not exposed to the sociology of metropolitan Manila fared no better than the non-Tagalogs who were similarly situated. The first president of the First Republic, Emilio F. Aguinaldo, and a few members of the Cabinet were not Tagalogs. They came from another linguistic-cultural region, Cavite, which was geographically in the periphery of metropolitan Manila. The revolutionary government, the short-lived First Republic, the American colonial administration, and the post-colonial government and nongovernment leadership were monopolized by the Tagalog-speaking. Next to Spanish and English, Tagalog became the

---

[8] One good source of information on the Spanish racially-based stratification system is the old Spanish era baptismal records and certificates. This writer's mother was classified as *meztiza* (half Spanish); a distant paternal uncle as *octeron* (one eighth Spanish blood); and a father of a colleague was *Indio Puro* (pure Indian). Unfortunately, many of the baptismal as well as civil vital records were destroyed during World War II.

lingua franca of the educated, the economic and political elite and the cosmopolitan. The current national language, "Pilipino", uses mostly Tagalog for its grammatical construction and incorporates native and foreign terms and words.

The Status of Philippine Women

The sex structure in the Philippines is egalitarian, and ascendancy is bilateral and can be extended indefinitely. Women had and continue to have equal status with men, although in law there are still some vestiges of former colonial domination. In the area of employment, as well as participation in economic, political and social activities, not only is there an absence of explicit discrimination against employment of women in any capacity, but women may have advantages over the men. Employed married women are entitled to forty to ninety days maternity leave with pay, without loss of seniority, in addition to regular sick and vacation leaves. Moreover, the recently amended labor code requires employers, at their own expense, to provide day care centers for women employees with children. Under the principle of equality between the sexes, the revised labor code also provides "paternity leaves" to husbands. However, the government has limited maternity leave rights to the first three children (or pregnancies) for demographic reasons, *i.e.,* to reduce the birth rate, which is one of the highest in the world.

Marriage and "homemaking" can be pursued simultaneously with a career or activities outside the home. In addition to statutes favoring the employment of women, the extended family system provides babysitters or surrogate parental care. The upper and upper middle classes can afford to hire servants, and those who cannot may use day care facilities.

The egalitarian status between the sexes predated contact with the West. In precolonial society, women slaves had the same status as male slaves, just as women in the noble class had the same status as men in the same class. In some instances, women assumed leadership positions in the society (Blair and Robertson, 1903:133-135). Nance (1972:219-240) reports that in many instances the spokesperson of the Tasadays was a woman. Agoncillo and Alfonso (1967:42) reported that:

> Women (Pilipino), before the coming of the Spaniards, enjoyed a unique position in society that their descendants during the Spanish occupation did not enjoy. Customary laws gave them the right to be equal to men, for they could own and inherit property, engage in trade and industry, and succeed to the chieftainship of a barangay in the absence of a male heir. Then, too, they had the exclusive right to give names to their children. As a sign of deep respect the men, when accompanying women, walked behind them.

Whether the Philippines (or parts of it) were once inhabited and ruled by matriarchies, as some writers contend, is still a subject of debate, since this contention had not yet been confirmed or challenged by evidence (Nakpil, 1978:20). However, a viable explanation for the equal status of the sexes in the Philippines may be the very high value society places on the family (nuclear and extended) and the larger group for individual survival and development. Any member of the family or group who is an actual or potential source of status and power for the family, regardless of gender, will be given due recognition, deference, opportunities and support to develop his/her potential. Any status and power achieved by the individual is shared by the group and individuals in the group. Conversely, any individual can also expect all types of support from the other members in times of need. For example, when a family can afford to send only one member to college, the whole family will invest their individual and collective efforts and resources in providing support for that person, regardless of the person's gender. In the case of a rape, it is considered not only an assault on a particular woman, but an affront against that woman's family and honor which may have to be rectified, if not by the law, then by the family.

Dimensions of Pilipino Personality and Interpersonal Behavior

The socialization towards group and communal welfare, and the protection of the group's interests *vis-a-vis* other groups, has to a certain extent affected the Pilipinos' personality and interpersonal behavior, particularly with those outside the family or group. Acceptance by the family is assumed. Interaction within the family is governed by norms, often accompanied by rituals which are determined by one's geneological and social position in the family.

Interpersonal relations outside one's family or group are often determined by or based on the Pilipino's concept of self-esteem, best represented by the term and concept of *hiya*. There is no exact equivalent of the term and its connotation in the English language. The most approximate equivalent would be what is commonly known as loss of face or shame. Although the Pilipino is psychologically and socially conditioned to behave as part of a group, he/she also values treatment of an individual as a separate person and as a member of a distinct group. What is therefore perceived as an affront or insult is resented and thus evokes anger not only by the individual's self-esteem and to the family's collective self-esteem, name and honor, both the individual and the family are placed in a position of hiya or loss of face (Bulatao, 1964:424-438).

The importance of self-esteem makes social acceptance a very highly valued social norm. Most societies place some value on social acceptance by other persons as a basis for interpersonal relations. In general, social acceptance is the norm that guides the social interaction of Pilipinos. Basically, this means accepting and therefore treating individuals for what they are, for what they think they are, or for what they claim to be. In empirical terms, this means that if a person claims he/she is a professor, then that person should be treated as such, regardless of any private reservations one has about the claim. To show some doubt in a covert manner or to fail to extend to that person the treatment expected would subject the "professor" to hiya. On the other hand, Pilipinos want to be treated as persons rather than as adjuncts to roles. They resent interaction based on a purely "official" or "business" basis.

Claims to status and power must be as realistic as possible. Dishonesty, deceit and false representations are resented and avoided. The concept of hiya acts as a built-in check against exaggerated claims. It is believed that by claiming less than what one really is, one can eventually be exalted for having been humble. However, claims that are beyond realities stand the risk of being uncovered, and the claimant humbled, which would subject the person and the family to hiya (Guthrie and Azores, 1968:57-59).

In general, social acceptance is reflected in the day to day social interaction, where maintenance of "smooth interpersonal relations" (SIR) is the norm. SIR is supposed to reduce interpersonal stresses by deemphasizing differences and by avoiding direct face to face confrontations. This means agreeing, or at least appearing not to disagree, in face to face situations or publicly, regardless of how one feels privately, thereby reducing tension, avoiding possible situations of interpersonal conflict and maintaining SIR. To disagree publicly in a face to face situation might subject the other person to hiya. Another illustration would involve "delicate" negotiations between two persons or groups, especially of different barangays. These negotiations might be for a personal loan or service, assistance in seeking a job, an approach for a group (power) alliance, or a daughter's hand in marriage. It is always desirable to have a third party or intermediary handle such negotiations. By avoiding a face to face situation, the petitioner does not have to risk hiya by "humbling" him/herself before somebody else. At the same time, if the need or request cannot be accommodated, then the second person is spared the ordeal of making the rejection directly, thereby preserving SIR and the self-esteem of all parties concerned.

Another form of which social acceptance is manifested is in the phenomenon of *pakikisama* or getting along with the group. A person who is not involved or shows indifference to the interests, welfare and activities of the group is viewed with suspicion and distrust, which is one manifestation of the emphasis of the supremacy of the group over the individual. An individual is therefore compelled to agree or go along with the group (or at least give that impression), since one of the possible consequences would be alienation from the group; a situation that most Pilipinos, or most people for that matter, dread (Guthrie and Azores, 1968:1-63; Lynch, 1970:1-75).

THE PILIPINOS IN THE UNITED STATES: CIRCA THE 1980s

Demographic, Social and Economic Characteristics

There were 774,652 Pilipinos in the United States in 1980 (*See,* Table 1), comprising 3.6 percent of the foreign born population in the U.S. This is more than twice the number in 1970 of 336,371 (U.S. Census of Population: 1970; Subject Reports PC(2)-1G. 1973:120). More than half (68.8%) lived in the West, of which 45.8 percent were in California and 16.9 percent were in Hawaii. Of the remainder, 10.9 percent resided in the South, 10.4 percent in

the Northcentral region and 9.9 percent in the Northeast. The majority
(64.1%) of the Pilipinos in the U.S. in 1980 were born outside the country,
mainly in the Philippines. Most (97.7%) belonged to 197,372 households, of
which about 10 percent were headed by women. The average size of the
Pilipino family in 1980 was four persons (U.S. Census of Population: 1980.
PC80-S1-12, December 1983:12; PC80-1-B1, May 1983:1-50; PC80-1-C1,
December 1983:10f, 17).

TABLE 1

Number of Pilipinos by Age Groups and Percentage of Female/Male
Distribution in the United States: 1980

Age Groups	Total Number (F & M)	Percent of: [a] Females	Males
Totals	774,652 (100%)	400,461 51.7%	374,191 48.3%
Under 5 years	69,022	48.6	51.4
05 to 09	72,519	48.3	51.7
10 to 14	67,253	48.3	51.7
15 to 19	62,165	48.9	51.1
20 to 24	61,861	53.1	46.9
25 to 29	76,472	58.0	42.0
30 to 34	83,353	58.9	41.1
35 to 39	67,947	56.8	43.2
40 to 44	51,470	53.5	46.5
45 to 49	34,111	52.7	47.3
50 to 54	28,730	54.6	45.4
55 to 59	23,633	56.7	43.3
60 to 64	18,858	57.0	43.0
65 to 69	21,837	41.4	58.6
70 to 74	19,523	29.0	71.0
75 years and older	15,898	26.3	73.7
Percent of those 16 years and older	71.4%	73.2%	69.4%
Median age	28.6	29.1	27.8

Source: U.S. Bureau of the Census. Census of Population: 1980. *PC-1-B1 General Characteristics
of the Population. United States Summary.* Washington, D.C.: United States Printing Office, May
1983:1-50.

Note: [a] Figures may not tally to 100% due to rounding.

Table 2 provides the educational characteristics of the Pilipinos in the United States in 1980. Note that Pilipino women had higher educational credentials than men. This is consistent with pre-immigration data (Chapter IV) and with the 1970 U.S. Census of Population (U.S. Census of Population; 1970:PC(2)-1G, 1973:135). At this point, it may be posited that these figures could be indicative of any one of a combination of the following factors: 1) women always constituted more than half of the immigrants admitted to the U.S. from the Philippines, before and after the 1965 Immigration Act; and 2) more than half of the Pilipinos in the U.S., in 1980 were foreign-born. (Immigration and Naturalization Service, 1961:31-32; 1966:39-40; 1971: 52-53; 1976:51-52; U.S. Census of Population: 1980. PC80-1-C1, December 1983:10f). This means that the high educational credentials of Pilipino women (and men) in the U.S., in 1980, were acquired prior to their immigration.

TABLE 2

Selected Educational Characteristics of Pilipinos Age
Twenty-five and Older in the United States: 1980

Selected Educational Characteristics	Total (M & F)	Male	Female	Percent of Females to Total (M & F)
Totals	100% (445,912)	100% (206,408)	100% (239,504)	53.7% —
Completed 8 years elementary grades only	2.5%	2.5%	2.5%	53.3
High school graduates	74.2	73.1	75.1	50.7
4 years college of more	37.0	32.2	41.2	59.8
Median school years completed	14.1	13.5	14.4	—

Source: U.S. Bureau of the Census. Census of Population: 1980. Characteristics of the Population, Vol. 1, Chapter C. *PC80-1-C1. General Social and Economic Characteristics, United States Summary.* December 1983:157.

In 1980, 95.2 percent of the civilian labor force (age 16 and older) were fully employed (94.9% of the men and 95.5% of the women). Table 3 provides the class of worker and type of industry, and Table 4 delineates their specific occupations. Of the few Pilipinos who were self-employed, many were physicians with private practices, a few were consultants and some owned gas stations. Unlike other Asians (*i.e.,* Chinese, Korean, Vietnamese, etc.), Pilipinos do not seem to go into retail or service businesses (Macaranas, 1984). Tables 3 and 4 seem to indicate that although Pilipinos do have high educational credentials, their occupations are somewhat in the lower technical and sales or service sector levels. This is especially so with regards to women.

TABLE 3

Class of Employment and Industry of Employed Pilipinos Age Sixteen and Older in Percentages and by Gender in the United States: 1980

Class of Worker and Industry	Total (M & F)	Male	Female	Percent of Females to Total (M & F)
Total employed	100% (361,469)	100% (170,417)	100% (191,052)	52.9% —
Private wage and salaried workers	79.1	78.1	79.9	53.4
Government (federal, state and local)	18.0	18.1	17.9	52.5
Self-employed	2.7	3.6	1.9	37.4
Unpaid family workers	0.2	0.1	0.3	71.6

Source: U.S. Bureau of the Census. Census of Population: 1980. Characteristics of the Population, Vol. 1, Chapter C. *PC80-1-C1. General Social and Economic Characteristics. United States Summary, December 1983:159.*

The data that a large number (25.1%) of Pilipinos are employed in top level occupations might be impressive within the context of affirmative action and the ideology that everyone, regardless of race, has an equal chance to get gainful employment. However, the data does not indicate how many of those employed in lower categories (*i.e.,* clerical, service workers, etc.), are under-employed or overeducated for the jobs in which they are able or allowed to work (Morales, 1974:82-89; 127-131). Indeed, the U.S. Commission on Civil Rights (USCCR), reported that, in general, minority groups and women were overqualified for their jobs when compared with white males (USCCR 1978:17-27, 89). Note that a large proportion of the Pilipino women are in occupations traditionally associated with women in the U.S. and elsewhere.

The median income of Pilipino families in the U.S. in 1979 was $26,687, and those of unrelated individuals age fifteen and older was $7,763. Their average incomes were $27,194 and $9,373, respectively. Although Pilipino women had higher educational credentials than Pilipino men and in many instances were employed proportionately in high-income occupations, their median income for 1979 was $4,268, while for men it was $8,109. Clearly, Pilipino women in the U.S., regardless of their high educational attainment, do not fare any better than their American "sisters" in the discriminatory rates between male and female earnings and wages.

Regarding housing, in 1980, there were 197,732, Pilipino occupied housing

TABLE 4

Occupation of Employed Pilipinos Age Sixteen and Older in the United States: 1980

Occupational Categories	Numbers Total (M & F)	Percent Distribution	Percent Females to Total (M & F)
Totals	361,469	100%	52.9% (191,052)
Managerial and professional specialty occupations	90,581	25.1	57.8
Executive, administrative and managerial occupations	27,937	7.7	43.5
Officials, administrators, public administration	655	0.2	31.3
Management related occupations	15,126	4.2	47.3
Professional specialty occupations	62,644	17.3	64.1
Engineers and natural scientists	10,466	2.9	21.1
Engineers	6,742	0.3	7.1
Health diagnostic occupations	11,233	3.1	36.1
Health assessment and treatment occupations	28,211	7.8	93.9
Teachers, librarians, counselors	7,371	2.8	72.4
Teachers, elementary and secondary schools	4,954	1.4	78.7
Technical, sales and administrative support occupations	120,399	33.3	64.9
Health technologists and technicians	10,665	3.0	78.4
Technologists and technicians, except health	11,061	3.1	28.8
Sales occupations	20,876	5.8	60.8
Supervisors and proprietors, sales occupations	1,948	0.5	39.1
Sales representatives, commodities and finance	5,275	1.5	38.5
Other occupations	13,653	3.8	72.5
Cashiers	6,182	2.6	80.0

TABLE 4 (Continued)

Occupation of Employed Pilipinos Age Sixteen and Older in the United States: 1980

Occupational Categories	Numbers Total (M & F)	Percent Distribution	Percent Females to Total (M & F)
Administrative support occupations, including clerical	77,797	21.5	69.2
Computer equipment operators	3,004	0.8	43.6
Secretaries, stenographers, typists	12,840	3.6	95.3
Financial records processing occupations	12,640	3.5	74.2
Mail and message distribution occupations	4,934	1.4	26.4
Service occupations	59,715	12.2	53.4
Private household occupations	1,937	0.9	88.3
Protective service occupations	3,519	1.0	10.4
Police and firefighters	740	0.2	–
Service occupations, except protective and household	54,259	15.0	54.9
Food service occupations	19,847	5.5	44.7
Cleaning and building service occupations	16,779	4.6	43.4
Farming, forestry and fishing occupations	10,125	2.8	22.4
Farm operators and managers	804	0.2	21.9
Farm workers and related occupations	9,106	2.5	22.7
Precision production, draft and repair occupations	29,882	8.3	21.3
Mechanics and repairers	8,433	2.3	4.3
Construction trades	6,908	1.9	2.7
Precision production occupations	14,470	4.0	40.0

TABLE 4 (Continued)

Occupation of Employed Pilipinos Age Sixteen and Older in the United States: 1980

Occupational Categories	Numbers Total (M & F)	Percent Distribution	Percent Females to Total (M & F)
Operators, fabricators and laborers	50,931	14.1	39.1
Machine operators and tenders, except precision	17,844	4.9	48.6
Fabricators, assemblers, inspectors and samplers	12,861	3.6	59.9
Transportation occupations	5,425	1.5	6.4
Motor vehicle operators	5,042	1.3	6.6
Material moving equipment operators	1,867	0.5	6.9
Handlers, equipment cleaners, helpers and laborers	12,850	3.6	25.1
Construction laborers	1,396	0.4	2.0
Freight, stock and material handlers	2,911	0.8	19.1

Source: U.S. Bureau of the Census. Census of Population: 1980. Characteristics of the Population, Vol. 1, Chapter C. *PC80-1C1. General Social and Economic Characteristics. United States Summary.* December 1983:160.

units (houses, condominiums and rentals). Over half (55.9%) of these were owned by the occupants. The median cost of owner-occupied houses was $79,400 and of condominiums was $71,000. The median monthly mortgage and rent were $106 and $227, respectively (1980 Census of Housing HC80-1-A1, May 1983:65).

Comparisons with Other Minorities

Table 5, shows the number and percentage of Pilipinos in the U.S. population in 1980 in comparison with other selected ethnic and/or racial groups. Like the other Asians (Japanese, Chinese, Korean, Asian Indians and Vietnamese), the Pilipinos were predominantly an urban population. Whereas in the 1970 Census Pilipinos comprised the smallest group among the "original" Asian (Japanese, Chinese and Pilipinos) immigrants, by 1980 they comprised the second largest group from Asia (U.S Census of Population: 1970 PC(2)-G1. July 1983:1, 60, 119). Historically, Asians came to the U.S. much later than the other minority groups. Yet, as will be shown, they seem to be "getting ahead" in the American system compared to the groups that preceeded them.

It has been commonly accepted that, barring any external barrier such as discrimination, persons with high educational credentials and a will to work hard have better chances of getting ahead in an industrial-technologial society such as the United States. At a glance, Tables 6-10 seem to indicate that this is the case for Asians with the exception of the Vietnamese. Among the Asians, the Vietnamese were the latest to arrive in the U.S. and were refugees rather than "voluntary" immigrants. U.S. laws covering refugees are indiscriminate with regard to the educational, occupational and socioeconomic class of the immigrants. On the other hand (as will be discussed later) current U.S. immigration laws pertaining to those other than refugees highly discriminate towards those with high educational and occupational credentials. However, while the Pilipinos have higher educational attainments than the Chinese and Japanese, and not withstanding the "special relations" between Pilipinos and Americans, Pilipinos do not seem to be doing as well as the other two Asian groups.

While large-scale statistical data such as in the tables are impressive, they tend to gloss over particular nuances. For example, the median and average incomes of certain groups tend to be raised by a few relatively highly paid exceptions (*e.g.*, physicians). Moreover, other data has consistently shown that white males with a high school education earn more than minority males and white and minority women with a college education. In fact, this is clear when income is measured by gender. All the women, regardless of ethnic/racial group and educational attainment, earned less (about half) than the men (U.S. Department of Labor, Bureau of Labor Statistics, September 1982: U.S. Bureau of the Census. Series P-16, No. 139, February 1983; U.S. Census of Population: 1980.PC80-1-C1. December 1983:51, 52, 53, 111, 125, 161).

Another example is the cost of housing, whereby the data indicate that the

TABLE 5

Population Size: Percentage Distribution to the Total Population of Ethnic/Racial Groups and Percentage Distribution of Urban (Female and Male) and Female Populations in the United States: 1980

Ethnic/Racial Groups	Totals: F & M; Urban and Rural	Percent of Totals of: Ethnic/ Racial Groups	Urban Population (F & M)	Female Population
U.S. Total (All Groups)	226,545,805	100% a	73.7%	51.4%
White	180,256,366	79.56	70.5	51.4
Black	26,104,173	11.52	85.3	52.8
Spanish Origin	8,506,108	3.75	73.7	50.8
American Indian	1,364,033	0.60	52.7	50.6
Chinese	806,040	0.35	97.0	49.3
Pilipino	774,652	0.34	92.4	51.7
Japanese	700,974	0.30	91.7	54.2
Asian Indian	361,531	0.16	92.8	48.3
Korean	354,593	0.15	93.0	58.3
Vietnamese	261,729	0.12	95.4	48.2
Hawaiian	166,814	0.07	82.1	50.7
Other (1) b	130,473	0.05	69.8 c	49.0
Other (2) d	6,758,319	2.98	90.1	49.0

Source: U.S. Bureau of the Census. Census of Poulation: 1980. *PC80-1B1 General Characteristics of the Population. United States Summary.* Washington, D.C.: U.S. Government Printing Office, May 1983: 1-20; 1-21.

Notes: a May not tally to 100% due to rounding.

b Other (1) are groups with less than 100 thousand population (female and male) listed separately by the Census, but lumped together in this table. They include: Eskimo (42,162): Aleut (14,205); Guamanian (32,158) and Samoan (41,948).

c Eskimos and Aleuts were predominantly rural, while Guamanians and Samoans were predominantly urban populations.

d Other (2) are those listed as "Other" by the Census.

Pilipinos and other Asians seem to have more expensive homes. However, their housing space is actually smaller than the whites, when the number of persons per unit space is taken into account. More than half of the Pilipinos reside in California and Hawaii, two states that are more notorious for expensive housing. Moreover, many of these owner-occupied houses may have been acquired in the middle and late 1970s when housing costs were rising. What seems most likely is that the Asians are actually paying more and

TABLE 6

Educational Characteristics by Percentages of Completed High School, Four Years of College or More and Median School Years Completed of Persons Age Twenty-five and Older from Selected Ethnic/Racial Groups in the United States: 1980

Selected Ethnic/Racial [a] Groups	Completed High School	Percentages of Completed 4 Years of College or More	Median School Years Completed
United States	66.5%	16.2%	12.5%
White	68.8	17.1	12.5
Black	51.2	8.4	12.0
Spanish Origin	44.0	7.6	10.8
American Indian	55.8	7.7	12.2
Chinese	71.3	36.8	13.4
Pilipino	74.2	37.0	14.1
Japanese	18.6	26.4	12.9
Asian Indian	80.1	51.9	16.1
Korean	76.1	33.7	13.0
Vietnamese	62.0	12.9	12.4
Hawaiian	68.4	9.6	12.4

Source: U.S. Bureau of the Census. Census of Population: 1980. Characteristics of the Population, Vol. 1, Chapter C. *PC80-1-C1. General Social and Economic Characteristics, United States Summary.* December 1983: 71, 98, 118, 157.

Note: [a] Excludes those listed as "Others" by the Census and those listed separately by ethnic/racial groups with less than 100,000 (male and female) populations. The latter include: Eskimo (42,162); Samoan (41,948); Guamanian (32,158); and Aleut (14,205).

buying smaller houses than the white majority. This is indicated by the high cost compared with the size and type of housing (1980 Census of Housing. HC80-1-A1. May 1983:9, 61, 62, 63).

SUMMARY

The Pilipinos come from a nation of islands in Southeast Asia. The majority of the population are basically of Malay stock with interminglings of Chinese, Spanish, Indian and American. Pilipinos value status and power. However, they try to achieve these through group rather than individual efforts - the struggle for life which includes attainment of status and power would be difficult, if not impossible, to attain by individual efforts. Hence, Pilipinos have been socialized to perceive themselves not only as unique individuals, but more importantly as part of a group which may extend beyond the nuclear family, demanding and in turn giving loyalty and allegiance. Although these societal arrangements are supposed to last a person's lifetime, one may belong to several groups throughout life; or even change allegiance to other nonfamily groups. Pilipinos fear alienation. Since Pilipino life has always been supported and controlled by the group, they become uncomfortable when acting individually. Geographic or social distance from families or groups result in more acute loneliness or homesickness, since they are separated from those whose presence ordinarily provide support and direction (Guthrie and Azores, 1968:9).

The social stratification in the Philippines may be summarized as follows: the Spaniards attempted to maintain power and rule through the existing power structure, except that they introduced a stratification system based on race and they centralized the economic, political, social and cultural activities in one area, Manila. This meant that those closest to the metropolitan center of the nation had more opportunities for advancement. At the end of colonial rule (by both Spain and the United States), the elite and their children

TABLE 7

Number of Civilian Labor Force and Percent Unemployed of Persons Age Sixteen and Older of Selected Ethnic/Racial Groups in the United States: 1979

Selected Ethnic/Racial Groups a	Civilian Labor Force	Percent Unemployed
United States	104,449,817	6.5%
White	89,191,895	5.8
Black	10,582,436	11.8
Spanish Origin	5,992,723	8.9
American Indian	556,776	13.0
Chinese	414,768	3.6
Pilipino	379,853	4.8
Japanese	394,511	3.0
Asian Indian	181,434	5.8
Korean	149,202	5.7
Vietnamese	87,951	8.2
Hawaiian	73,531	7.0

Source: U.S. Bureau of the Census. Census of Population: 1980. Characteristics of the Population, Vol. 1, Chapter C. *PC80-1-C1 General Social and Economic Characteristics. United States Summary.* December 1983: 26, 119, 151, 159.

Note: a Excludes those listed as "Others" by the Census and those listed separately by ethnic/racial groups with less than 100,000 (male and female) population. The latter include Eskimo (42,162); Samoan (41,948); Guamanian (32,158); and Aleut (14,205).

TABLE 8

Median and Mean Annual Incomes of Families and Unrelated Individuals, Age Fifteen and Older of Selected Ethnic/Racial Groups in the United States: 1979

Selected Ethnic/Racial Groups [a]	Family Median	Mean	Unrelated Median	Individuals Mean
United States	$19,917	$23,092	$6,695	$9,282
White	20,835	24,166	7,036	9,695
Black	12,598	15,684	4,738	6,916
Spanish Origin	14,712	17,263	5,391	7,217
American Indian	13,678	16,499	4,810	6,999
Chinese	22,559	26,600	5,147	8,436
Pilipino	23,687	27,194	7,763	9,373
Japanese	27,354	30,527	7,912	10,067
Asian Indian	24,993	29,591	5,890	9,565
Korean	20,459	24,670	4,632	7,056
Vietnamese	12,840	15,527	3,374	5,836
Hawaiian	19,196	21,495	5,915	8,357

Source: U.S. Bureau of the Census. Census of Population: 1980. Characteristics of the Population, Vol. 1, Chapter C. *PC80-1-C1. General Social and Economic Characteristics. United States Summary.* December 1983: 51, 52, 53, 111, 125, 161.

Note: [a] Excludes those listed as "Others" by the Census and those listed separately by ethnic/racial groups with less than 100,000 (male and female) population. The latter include: Eskimo (42,162); Samoan (41,948); Guamanian (32,158); and Aleut (14,205).

TABLE 9

Median Costs of Owner-Occupied Housing Units and Condominiums and Monthly
Rents of Selected Ethnic/Racial Groups in the United States: 1980

Selected Ethnic/Racial Groups [a]	Owner-Occupied Housing Units	Costs of Condominiums	Monthly Rent
United States	$47,200	$59,600	$198
White	48,600	59,600	208
Black	27,200	42,700	156
Spanish Origin	44,700	56,500	188
American Indian	34,400	50,000	171
Chinese	89,600	82,300	221
Pilipino	79,400	71,000	227
Japanese	93,100	85,500	253
Asian Indian	74,300	59,400	245
Korean	86,100	75,500	250
Vietnamese	56,800	61,300	235
Hawaiian	79,200	84,700	238

Source: U.S. Bureau of the Census. 1980 Census of Housing. Characteristics of Housing Units,
Vol. 1, Chapter A. *HC80-1-A1. General Housing Characteristics, United States Summary.* May
1983: 9, 61, 62, 63.

Note: [a] Excludes those listed as "Others" by the Census and those listed separately by ethnic/racial
groups with less than 100,000 (male and female) populations. The latter include: Eskimo
(42,162); Samoan (41,948); Guamanian (32,158); and Aleut (14,205).

(whether in the capital or not) and those exposed to the urban centers had
greater advantages. In effect, having been a *Manileno* rather than ethnic
natality proved advantageous in a modernizing society.

From the 1980 U.S. Census of Population it was determined that Pilipinos
comprised the second largest Asian group in the United States, although
smaller than other minority groups such as black, Hispanic and American
Indian. They are mainly concentrated on the West Coast, particularly in
California and Hawaii and are a predominantly urban and young population.
Except for the Asian Indians, the Pilipinos had the highest educational
credentials among all the selected ethnic/racial groups included in this study.
Their socioeconomic status as measured by labor force participation, income
(family and individual), housing and poverty levels is higher than other
groups that preceeded them to the U.S. Nevertheless, as will be discussed
elsewhere, the impressive aggregate data on socioeconomic status may hide
individual nuances, showing that the Pilipino's problems are no different than
those of other minority groups. One such case is that of Pilipino women.

TABLE 10

Percentage of Poverty Levels of Families and Unrelated Individuals of Selected
Ethnic/Racial Groups in the United States: 1979

Selected Ethnic/Racial Groups [a]	Families	Unrelated Individuals
United States	9.6%	25.1%
White	7.0	22.6
Black	26.5	39.7
Spanish Origin	21.3	35.9
American Indian	23.7	38.6
Chinese	10.5	33.0
Pilipino	6.2	23.2
Japanese	4.2	24.4
Asian Indian	7.4	27.8
Korean	13.1	36.1
Vietnamese	35.1	48.7
Hawaiian	14.3	33.2

Source: U.S. Bureau of the Census. Census of Population: 1980. Characteristics of the
Population, Vol. 1, Chapter C. *PC80-1-C1. General Social and Economic Characteristics, United
States Summary.* December 1983: 63, 126, 162.

Note: [a] Excludes those listed as "Others" by the Census and those listed separately by ethnic/
racial groups with less than 100,000 (male and female) populations. The latter include: Eskimo
(42,162); Samoan (41,948); Guamanian (32,158); and Aleut (14,205).

Notwithstanding the fact that they have higher educational credentials than
the men, their incomes are almost half that of Pilipino men, a situation
prevailing in the system affecting women of all ethnic/racial groups.

This chapter examined selected aspects of the Philippines; social and other
characteristics of the Philippine social structure and Pilipinos; and some data
on Pilipinos in the United States, as reported in the 1980 U.S. Census of
Population. The next chapter will examine some macro historical, economic,
political and cultural structures in the Philippines, and the United States and
the world that precipitated the immigration of Pilipinos to the U.S.

3. *Historical and Structural Components of Pilipino Immigration to the United States*

One of the contentions of this work is that the immigration process was, and still is, precipitated by macro structures across time and space over which most voluntary immigrants had or have little or no control. Exceptions were made for war and political refugees whose migrations were even less voluntary and under more traumatic and tragic circumstances. However, within the context of this work, it can be posited that, with the exception of blacks, native Americans and some of the Spanish-speaking in the West and Southwest, most Americans are descended from or are refugees in one form or another.

Moreover, the historically developed macro structures that have precipitated the immigration of people to the United States to a great extent set the tone and constraints under which the immigrants interacted with those that preceeded them and their institutions. Although blacks and other nonwhite immigrants brought or induced to come to the U.S. for similar reasons and were treated similarly, each group reacted in its own particular way.

This chapter suggests several major factors critical to the understanding of Pilipino immigration to the United States and subsequent patterns of interaction with Americans and American institutions. One, discussed in the preceeding chapter, is the changing patterns and contours of Philippine social structure and interpersonal behavior; second is the changing relationship of the people to the land and the geopolitical structures in the Philippines; third is the multidimensional nature of the Philippines under Spain and the United States, and the resulting status of that country in an international network of relationships; fourth is the changing economic and political structures in the United States that influenced that country's policies toward certain types of immigrants; and fifth is the changing bilateral and multilateral networks of relationships between the United States and immigrants' countries of origin. In other words, these factors help explain the similarities and differences of the Pilipino experience compared with that of the Chinese and Japanese immigrants.

THE CHANGING STRUCTURES IN THE PHILIPPINES: PRE-COLONIAL, COLONIAL, POST-COLONIAL AND NEO-COLONIAL

Among the countries in the region, the Philippines had the longest colonial experience under Western powers. It was a Spanish colony for three centuries and an American colony for approximately half a century. The Americans referred to the country as a U.S. territory and/or "ward" but never as a colony. As to whether the Philippines continued to be a "neo-colony" of the U.S. long after its independence in 1946 is still the subject of debate in the Philippines and elsewhere. At this point, suffice it to say that Pilipino immigrants to the U.S. come from a society with a long colonial history, of which almost half a century was with the United States.

The Spanish Colonial Experience

Political Restructuring. The Philippines was a colony of Spain from 1565 to 1898. The Spanish explorers and colonizers did not "discover" an Asian nation state or empire characterized by advanced settlements with large public buildings and temples, nor a nationwide political system. What they found and tried to rule for three centuries were scattered autonomous settlements (barangays) and kingdoms (confederations of barangays), allied or at war with each other, and trading with neighbors such as China, India, Indochina and some Arab traders from the southern part of the archipelago. In each of these settlements, however, they found an elaborate stratification system, codified laws and a system of writing which resembled a combination of Hindu sanskrit and Arabic script.

The Spanish attempted to use the classic colonial pattern of administration by superimposing their rule over the existing political structure. However, the absence of a national power structure made this task difficult. What facilitated the political and administrative unification and colonization of the islands was the introduction of a common religion, the Catholic faith. Except for the Muslims in the south, this was almost universally accepted by the natives as manifested by the number of people baptized to the faith (Agoncillo and Alfonso, 1967:23-38). Unlike the British, the Dutch or the French, one of the aims of Spanish colonization was the propagation of the Catholic faith. Every Spanish expedition and subsequent colonial administration was invariably accompanied by missionaries and ecclesiastical authority as part of the colonial administration. Thus, church and state became inseparable in Spanish colonial administration, although at various times leaders from the two institutions were often engaged in conflicts of power.

Spanish colonial settlements required the establishment of *pueblos* (towns) which became the centers of political, civil, military and ecclesiastical administrations. Facing each other in the town plaza were the church, town hall, local garrison and principal homes of Spanish and local elites, expanding into regular grid patterns for the rest of the population. This meant that the pre-Spanish scattered settlements of the barangays had to be brought together "under the church bells" which not only tolled the hours of worship, but also served as the town time and alarm systems (Corpus, 1965:25-27). The Spaniards were conscientious urban planners. From the first settlement in Cebu to Manila, every Philippine town was carefully planned and laid out using the "plaza complex" (Hollnstiener, 1969:147-174).

Corpus, in his work "The Philippines" (1965:27-28), capsulized the Spanish colonial, political and administrative rule of the Philippines, and how the Pilipinos responded:

> The old barangays and their members were brought bodily into the new scheme of municipal organization. The folk of the pueblo were divided into barangays, each under its own head or *cabeza*. This traditional leader therefore became an administrative functionary of the colonial regime and his position remained hereditary, as before. The cabeza's chief responsibility was to collect the levies, called *tributos*, from each adult member of the barangay and to see to it that the personal labor services called *polos y servicios* - a system of forced labor for supposed public purposes - were rendered. In recognition of this service and of this social status, the cabeza was exempted from the tributo and first sons were given the same exemption. The cabeza of the town collectively made up the *principalia* or leading citizens. From among them the *gobernadorcillo* or "little governor" was chosen as town head.

> The principalia as a local aristocracy became a durable social institution. The cabezas and the gobernadorcillo did not count for much in the eyes of the Spanish colonial community. They were ill recompensed for their onerous responsibilities, terrorized by the Spanish friar who was the parish priest, and victimized by the Spanish provincial governor and his retinue of fellow Spaniards. In the eyes of their fellow natives, however, their sociopolitical status remained as exalted as before, and some of them succumbed to the temptation of emulating their Spanish superiors, indulging in graft - from the tribute collections and other sources - on their own account. Their role in the large society of Filipinos and Spaniards was that of political shock absorbers and cultural middlemen. It turned out to be an important role. The demands of the Spanish officials and friars were transmitted to the masses of the Filipinos through the principalia. Since these demands were invariably burdensome and vexatious, the principalia justified them to their own people; in turn, they represented the natives' difficulties to the rulers. It was a natural process, and there was nothing highflown and noble about it. To preserve their status with the masses below, the cabezas and gobernadorcillos sought in effect to moderate the regime's impositions. To preserve their prerogatives in the colonial order, they cooperated and collaborated. The outcome was a *modus vivendi* between the native community and the Spanish community. In practice, the Filipino masses complied incompletely or only externally - evaded where possible - the rigorous exactions of the colonial order. The friars and officials of the

regime tried to get more compliance, but accepted what they in fact got. It was not a perfect relationship, but it could have been much worse. The Spanish occupation rested, and lasted, on this equilibrium.

For their part, the ordinary people were of no consequence to the Spaniards except as the source of revenue. The avenues of social mobility were closed. Politics was not available to them. Education was rudimentary and intended for nothing but unquestioning acceptance of the friar's interpretation of Christian faith and morals. Economic entrepreneurship was impossible in the provinces; government policies reduced them to stagnation until the later eighteenth century. In the cities, the Chinese, who had been coming in increasing numbers as resident craftsmen and traders, monopolized the service trades. Indeed, a perverted system of values developed in which assignment to menial tasks in the service of the friar or of some Spaniard was accorded social distinction - but even these lowly services were reserved for the families of the principalia. The colonial order froze the Filipino masses to permanent impotence.

A significant aspect of Spanish colonial rule was the power of the clergy, particularly the friars. They were directly responsible to the crown through their mother organizations either in Spain or Rome and not to the Spanish colonial civil and military administrators. In some instances, they served as buffers between the natives and the abuses of other Spaniards, although it was often in the spirit of protecting God's "innocent little children". In other instances, they were the Spanish colonial authority in the towns which did not have any civil or military administrators. The friars became landlords under the *encomeinda* system of land ownership. Many of the secular clergy and religious orders became so powerful, that they often clashed with the civil and military colonial authorities for political and economic power. The friars became oppressive landlords, political and economic reactionaries who opposed any reforms that the more liberal colonial authorities wanted to introduce. Thus, towards the end of the Spanish colonial rule, the friars, together with the *guardia civil* (civil guard, a paramilitary national police), became the most hated personalized symbols of oppression (Agoncillo, 1956:135; 152-154; 168-169).

Economic Ramifications. One of the most lasting, if not permanent, effects of Spanish colonization was the restructuring of the economic systems of the Philippines. Spain introduced the Pilipinos to the money economy and to a wider network of world trade, compared to the pre-Spanish barter trade with Asian neighbors. Any form of production (agriculture, fishing and cottage industries) was controlled by the colonial government. Foreign trade was a government monopoly and local retail trade was relegated to the Chinese under the careful supervision of the authorities. In 1834, European firms were allowed to trade in the Philippines.

For more than two centuries, the principal domestic and international economic activity of the Philippine colony was the Manila-Acapulco (Mexico) or galleon trade as it was commonly known. It followed the monopolistic mercantilism typical of colonial economic activity. Only Spaniards could engage in wholesale or international commerce. Even they were restricted from trading directly with any Asian countries or with the natives. They had to trade through the government agencies or through agencies designated by the authorities. The Chinese and other Asian traders brought their goods to designated outlets where the Spanish traders bought and resold them to Mexico via the port of Acapulco for as much as 100 percent profit. Only a few Philippine goods such as cordage, hemp and handwoven textiles, and towards the end of Spanish rule Philippine sugar and tobacco were exported. Most of the goods shipped through Manila via the galleon trade were silks from China, rugs and carpets from Persia and spices from India and East Indies. There was only one galleon on the Manila-Acapulco and one on the Acapulco-Manila run. Since there were more goods to be shipped and traded than space available on the trips, getting shipping space on the galleons became highly competitive and a source of corruption.

The profits from the trade helped finance some of the public works and charities in the colonies. However, it became such a lucrative undertaking that it soon bred corruption among the Spanish colonizers. Colonial administrators (civil, military and ecclesiastical) soon neglected their duties and concentrated their efforts on getting their "piece of the action" from the galleon trade. The Pilipinos benefited least from the trade; in fact, it was profitably conducted at their expense. First, the galleons were built in the Philippines by conscript labor. Second, the Philippine products included in the trade were bought cheaply and resold to Mexico at tremendous profits, all accruing to the Spanish traders and colonizers. Third, since the Spaniards were too busy concentrating on the galleon trade, they failed to notice, much less control, the increasing participation and later monopoly of the Chinese in retail trading and money lending businesses. These had a long-run negative effect on the development of native business and economic independence (Corpus, 1965:30-31; Agoncillo and Alfonso, 1967:89-93; 109-110).

Spanish agricultural policy was restrictive, oppressive and exploitive, although a beneficial effect of Spanish rule was the introduction of new methods of farming and scientific agriculture. The immediate beneficiaries of such innovations were not the Pilipinos however. Among the agricultural innovations was the introduction of cash crops such as sugar, tobacco and abaca for hemp. Not only were the Pilipinos limited in their marketing through Spanish monopoly, they were also prohibited from cultivating other crops that were not within the scheme of the colonial agroeconomic system. Pilipinos were reluctant to produce more than they needed for subsistence and what was required of them, for fear that the fruits of their efforts would not be fairly compensated by the monopolized marketing system, or that they would be confiscated by a local colonial administrator or friar (Agoncillo and Alfonso, 1967:110-112).

The most damaging innovation was the restructuring of the land use and tenure system by the introduction of the *encomienda* patterned after the feudal system in Europe. The encomienda was a royal title to large tracts of land, not of ownership, but of the right to collect tribute and benefit from the inhabitants of the land covered by the title in return for keeping the peace and propagating the faith. Thus, in addition to producing for their own needs, the people in the encomiendas had to produce for the needs of the *encomiendero* which included so many days of free labor per week in whatever agricultural or industrial enterprise the encomienda was engaged. The encomiendas were given to Spaniards in recognition of services to the crown, and to the diocesan Church and religious orders for their maintenance in lieu of subsidies from the royal treasury and/or from Rome. The latter encomiendas became notoriously known as the "friar lands" and these were coveted by American agrobusiness and the native rich. They were, of course, the most fertile and beautiful lands.

The system became so oppressive that towards the end of colonial rule it had to be abolished; that is, the titles to the encomiendas could not be inherited by heirs when the original grantees passed on. But by that time, the encomienderos or their heirs were too economically and politically powerful to be dislodged from "their" land. Thus, what was intended to be a trust on royal lands became, in fact, titles of ownership. Since the majority of the Pilipinos were and still are dependent on agriculture as their main means of livelihood, the encomienda system, more than anything else, had the most lasting effects on individual, family and societal economics. From a combination of communal and private landownership, producing what they needed and for barter, the Pilipinos became tenant sharecroppers in what was once their own land, not even getting a fair share of products. Moreover, the encomienda was the precursor of *hacienda* (plantation type) agriculture, which continued to be a major social problem in the country until the 1970s (Corpus, 1965:32-34; Agoncillo and Alfonso, 1976:85-86; 525-526; 596-598).

Reforms, Nationalism, Revolution and a Taste of Independence. In his work *The Revolt of the Masses* (1956), Teodoro A. Agoncillo contends that the major cause of the Philippine revolution against Spain was economic, and that it was initially and principally a plebian movement. There had been, throughout centuries of Spanish colonial rule, sporadic uprisings throughout the islands. In fact, the "discoverer" of the Philippines, Fernando Magallanes, a Portuguese in the service of Spain, was killed in 1521 on the island of Mactan by the island's king, Lapu-lapu, who refused to be baptized in the new religion much less acknowledge the sovereignty of a foreign ruler. None of these oppositions against Spain could be considered a national movement, much less a revolution, until 1896. The middle and upper classes considered the oppressive colonial administration as abuses of local officials and reactionary elements among the clergy, rather than as inherent matters in a colonial structure.

The initial "nationalist" movement was directed at effecting reforms in the colonial administration, among which was the perception and demand that the Philippines be made a Spanish province (instead of a colony) and be represented in the Spanish Cortes (Parliament). The middle and upper classes suffered economic and political deprivation compared to the Spaniards. Reforms would have given them a more equitable position. It was the masses who suffered almost absolute economic deprivation. For them, these reforms meant raising the status of some Pilipinos to the level of the Spaniards, without affecting their lives. The only escape from their economic and social bondage was through complete political independence, whereby as a free people they could assume control of the means of livelihood and determine their own fate. It took the *Katipunan* (KKK) to galvanize these individual and regional aspirations into a national movement and revolution.

To understand the Katipunan is to understand the Philippine revolution. Katipunan is short for *Kataastaasan Kagalang-galangan Katipunan ng mga Anak ng Bayan.* Freely translated, it means the Society of the Highest and Most Illustrious Sons of the Motherland. It was founded by Andres Bonifacio, a man of very little education with lower class origins. Compared to other organizations such as the *Lega Filipina* (Philippine League), which opposed abuses in the colonial administration, the Katipunan was a radical organization in that it was based on the belief that the only way out of oppression was through political independence by armed conflict. Its internal structure and administration followed closely that of freemasonry, replete with secret initiation and other rites.

The Katipunan became the first national movement in that it attracted membership from all regional-linguistic groups as well as a few from the middle classes and intelligentsia. Some of the middle classes opposed it while most watched with interest from a safe distance. The rich and church authorities opposed it; the civil and military authorities viewed it with some apprehension, but did not consider the movement serious enough to be given more attention than similar ones in the past, to the chagrin of the ecclesiastical authorities who demanded that drastic measures be taken against the Katipunan. For the first time in Philippine history, the natives were opposing and fighting a common oppressor, not as Tagalogs, Visayans or Ilocanos, but as Pilipinos. To be a *Katipunero* was to be a revolutionary.

The first open armed conflict with the Spanish authorities came in the last week of August 1896, and quickly spread throughout the country. The neutral or even pro-Spanish position of the rest of the middle class and the rich did not save them from retaliation by the Spanish authorities. As far as the latter were concerned all Pilipinos were suspect. This was further exacerbated by the fact that the Katipuneros, upon failure to get the voluntary support of the rich, tried to implicate them with the movement before the Spanish authorities.[9]. In the meantime, political reforms came, but it was a matter of too little, too late. The Katipunan denounced the reforms and the struggle continued. Spanish resistance in the provinces started to collapse. More of the population, including intellectuals, middle class, rich and progressive and liberal elements in the European community, began to support it.

[9] The strategy was to manufacture evidence that the rich Pilipinos were secretly supporting the revolution and leak this to the Spanish authorities. Based on experience the *Katipurneros* (or revolutionaries) were sure that the Spanish authorities would not bother to examine the veracity of the alleged support. Therefore, Spanish action against the rich would leave the latter no alternative but to support the movement. As it turned out, this strategy was not even necessary, since the Spaniards struck back at all Pilipinos, rich and poor (Agoncillo, 1956:112-116; 143-146).

On March 22, 1897, a convention was called in which the Katipunan (as a secret society) was replaced by a revolutionary government; Emilio F. Aguinaldo was elected president and Andres Bonifacio, director of interior. The convention resulted in a power struggle between factions in the revolutionary government, which resulted in the trial and execution of Andres Bonifacio for treason on May 10, 1897 (Agoncillo and Alfonso, 1976:213-217).

On June 12, 1898, the independence of the Philippines was declared at Cawit, Cavite. On June 18 and 23, the Revolutionary Congress convened at the church in Malolos, Bulacan, and the Malolos Constitution, patterned after the French and U.S. Constitutions, was adopted. The civil government under the Republic was operating in most of the country, while the symbolic remnants of Spanish rule were surrounded and besieged in Manila. Spanish rule of the Philippines was coming to an end when the Spanish-American war broke out, and the American Asiatic Squadron, under the command of Commodore George Dewey, sailed into Manila Bay on May 1, 1898.

Highlights and Implications of Spanish Colonization. Although Spain's motives for colonizing the Philippines may have been the same as those for the American continent, the results differed. The geographical, social and cultural heterogenity of the Philippine archipelago made the administration of the colonies difficult. Moreover, compared with South America, the Philippines had not been as profitable to the business interests of the crown. The only substantial source of revenue was the foreign trade monopoly and limited exports of cash crops. The resistance of the Pilipinos to produce agricultural and light industrial products for the benefit of the colonizers, the corruption of colonial officials and the increasing cost of maintaining peace and order contributed to making the Philippine colony an economic burden on the Spanish government towards the end of the 19th century (Agoncillo and Alfonso, 1967).

Furthermore, the Philippines was considered the last frontier of the Spanish Empire. It was such an undesirable place that Spaniards of "good quality" refused to go there and the posting of Spaniards (civil, military and church officials) to the colony was often a form of punishment or demotion (Abella, 1971). The colony was not even administered directly from Spain, but rather indirectly through Mexico, and the Spanish governor-general was responsible to the viceroy of Mexico instead of to the sovereign, although towards the end of Spanish rule the situation changed.

Except for its African colonies, the Philippines was the only Spanish colony where the native population outnumbered the Spanish population at the end of Spanish rule. At the turn of the nineteenth century, there were only 4,000 Spaniards and mestizos, compared with 2,500,000 natives. At the time Spain left the Philippines, less than one percent of the population was Spanish, the rest were natives and other races, such as the Chinese (Abella, 1971).

The impact of the Spanish on Pilipino culture was minimal compared to its impact on South America. Spanish language and cultural influences were limited to a minority among the urban population, although they filtered down to the rest of the population in one form or another. However, Spanish penetration into the native social structures, institutions, values and norms took on some form of cross-cultural detente. The observations of Phelan in *Hispanization of the Philippines* describes the general overall effect of Spanish colonization on Pilipino culture (Phelan, 1959:26):

>...The Filipinos were no mere passive recipients of the cultural stimulus created by the Spanish conquest. Circumstances gave them considerable freedom in selecting their response to Hispanization. Their responses varied all the way from acceptance to indifference and rejection... [and] they adapted many Hispanic features to their own indigenous culture. Preconquest society was not swept away by the advent of the Spanish regime...

>...significant elements of the old culture blended into the new society emerging under Spanish auspices, and in many cases took forms contrary to the wishes of the new regime... Although partially Hispanized, they never lost that Malaysian stratum which to this day remains the foundation of their culture.

The most significant impact of Spanish colonization was economic and political. The Spaniards restructured the ecological balance between the people and the environment. From an economic system based on subsistence and a little surplus for trade by autonomous settlements, the islands became an agricultural factory in order to sustain the colonial government, which also linked the island to an international commercial network. Instead of improving the economic lot of the Pilipinos, the international commercial linkages subjected them to further exploitation. In addition to producing to sustain the colonial government, the Pilipinos had to produce more to supply the requirements of the colonizer's international trade activities. The Spanish colonial economic system also contributed to the development of an economic and political elite and bourgeois who were slightly better off than the rest of the population. The majority of the people became indentured sharecroppers and urban proletariats.

The political effects of Spanish colonization of the Philippines resulted in an historial geopolitical phenomenon which the Spaniards could not have planned, much less desired. The urbanization of the islands, the centralized political, military, civil and ecclesiastical administrative structure, combined with universal exploitation and opposition of the natives, led to the development of racial and national consciousness from among an ethnically heterogeneous people living in autonomous settlements. The empirical manifestation of this consciousness was a national revolution which ended Spanish colonial rule and gave birth to a nation - the Philippines.[10]

---

[10]As noted earlier, the Philippines was named after Philip II of Spain. Since its independence and until its legislature was abolished by the current military regime, several attempts had been made to change the country's name to one that removes any foreign vestiges and reflects a nationalist character. All of these attempts failed. For one thing, any proposed name that reflected one of the regional-linguistic groups was opposed by other regional-linguistic groups. Besides, as cynics pointed out, any native or nationalistic nomenclature for the Philippines would be more symbolic than real.

The American Colonial Experience

The Spanish-American War (1898), in which the ostensible reason for American involvement was to help the Cubans gain their independence, gave the United States the opportunity to expand its "sphere of influence" in the Pacific area (Agoncillo and Alfonso, 1967:226-241). The Treaty of Paris on December 10, 1898 ended the Spanish-American War and ceded the Philippines to the U.S. in exchange for 25 million dollars. However, possession of the Islands by the U.S. was resisted by Pilipinos and it took four years of savage guerilla-type war before the entire country was relatively pacified (Francisco, 1973:2-16; Miller, 1982). The principal opposition came from the "anti-imperialists" who based their opposition on moral and constitutional grounds. They were joined by those who even had less concern for the fate of the Pilipinos. Among them were agricultural interests who feared competition from Philippine agricultural products such as sugar and coconut oil; organized labor which was apprehensive about the possible entry of cheap labor; and the chronic racists who were appalled at the notion that those brown people might become U.S. citizens and might dilute the purity of the Anglo Saxon race (Grunder and Livezey, 1951:27-50; Wolfe, 1960:141-219).

The armed resistance by the Pilipinos combined with the opposition in the U.S. influenced the abandonment of any aims of annexing the Philippines to the U.S. The official American position on the Philippines was that the U.S. was to prepare the country for independence which included development of military capabilities so that it could defend itself from other countries' aggression. The political and economic strategy was to have a friendly ally in Asia that could be depended upon to provide "coaling stations" for U.S. warships and a bridge to the Asian trade market. President McKinley assuaged the racist elements by emphasizing that the U.S. aims for the Philippines were economic rather than social assimilation; through a delegation of Methodist clergy he told the U.S. Protestant Church that it was the duty of the United States to christianize the Pilipinos (who had been Catholics for three centuries) (Grunder and Livezey, 1959:27-50; Wolfe, 1960:173-176). In the meantime, the military commanders, and later military governors, were crushing the armed resistance of the Pilipinos. Civil government was restored to pacified areas, with Pilipinos who took the oath of allegiance to the U.S. taking the reins of government, except the military and police. The Philippine Supreme Court was restored in which the majority, including the Chief Justice, was Pilipino.

The administration of the Philippines was removed from the military and on July 4, 1901, William Howard Taft, who later became the 27th President of the United States, took his oath of office as the first civil governor general of the Philippines before the Chief Justice of the Philippine Supreme Court, Señor Cayetano Arellano. Thus the official American policy of developing the Philippines for its eventual "independence" was set into motion (Grunder and Livezey, 1951:67-83).

Political Ramifications of the U.S. Policies and Administration. The announced policy for the Philippines, followed by acts implementing that policy, raised the questions of how and when the independence was to be achieved and how to maximize Pilipino participation in the U.S. administration of the islands. Restoration of the civil government was followed by "Filipinization" of the Philippine government. Basic individual rights to life, property, expression and political activities (not contrary to the U.S. policy) were guaranteed. In 1902, the Organic Act ratified all previous executive orders and instructions regarding U.S. administration of the Philippines. In 1907, an elective Philippine Assembly was established; this later became the lower legislative body and the appointed Philippine Commission became the upper legislative body. The latter was expanded and Pilipino members outnumbered the Americans. The task of pacifying the islands and maintaining peace and order nationwide was turned over to the newly organized Philippine Constabulary, composed of Americans and Pilipinos, which later became an all Pilipino establishment.

In the United States, the continued U.S. presence in the Philippines and the manner by which the U.S. was administering the islands continued to be a political issue. By and large, the Democrats, regarded as "anti-imperialists", were the defenders of Philippine interests while the Republicans pursued an imperialist position. However, within each party were those who pursued U.S interests at the expense of the Pilipinos and those who were on the opposite side. Any actions by the U.S. government favoring Pilipinos and the Philippines were accomplished during Democrat administrations and/or when they controlled the U.S. Congress (Grunder and Livezey, 1951:85; 146-209; Wolfe, 1960).

The Cultural Impact of the U.S. Presence: "Americanizing" the Philippines. Among the declared policies of the U.S. for the Philippines was the education of Pilipinos and their preparation for self-government. These were carried out principally through a massive education program. A nationwide public school system patterned after the American model was established. The first teachers, in a way the precursors of the Peace Corps, were known and remembered with nostalgia as the "Thomasites".[11]

In addition, the already existing nongovernment schools were likewise Americanized. Part of this thrust was the use of English as the medium of instruction from the first grade through higher education. The first textbooks were American. Later books reflected Philippine characteristics, but idealized American models, from the family to government and economics. Values and norms were likewise affected. To prefer traditional or native norms and values was considered a sign of illiteracy. Being an educated Pilipino meant preferring apple pie in a country where there are no apples and wearing American suits while the temperatures never went lower than seventy degrees Fahrenheit. American political/historical figures (Washington, Lincoln, etc.) were idealized and Philippine patriots who fought for their country's independence were

---

[11] Most of the first American public school teachers and civil servants "volunteered" for the "hazardous" job of "educating the natives". Their service to the Philippines assumed missionary dimensions. One of the first and largest contingents came on the troop ship St. Thomas, hence the "Thomasites".

portrayed as "bandits" "insurgents" and "hostiles".

The Americanization of Pilipinos, whether by design or accident, began to have these results and they impinged not only on the native culture but also on the economic, political and world outlook of Pilipinos as well. American models, whether in government, manner of dress, or lifestyle, became the ideal, whereas anything Pilipino or Asian was considered outmoded or inferior. Most of the urban Pilipinos and to some extent even those in the countryside, regardless of their social and economic status, were becoming cultural hybrids. Aping American lifestyles meant desiring American made consumer products - not just similar products manufactured in the Philippines, but those with the label "made in U.S.A". The Pilipinos, whether they could afford it or not, were becoming a consumer oriented society. In other words, the little brown people were being converted from *homines socialis* to *homines economicus,* sometimes at great social and cultural cost. Rizal's lamentations of the Westernization of Pilipinos may have been overstated as far as Spanish influence was concerned. However, these prophesied the effects that America had on Pilipinos half a century after he wrote that the Pilipinos...

>...gradually lost their ancient traditions, their recollections - they forgot their writings, their songs, their poetry, their laws, in order to learn by heart other doctrines which they did not understand; other ethics, other tastes, different from those inspired in their race by their climate and way of thinking. Then there was a falling off, they lowered in their own eyes, they became ashamed of what was distinctly their own in order to admire and praise what was foreign and incomprehensible; their spirit was broken and they acquiesced.[12]

Economic Ramifications. While U.S. official political policy and programs for the Philippines had been established, the economic ramifications of the U.S. presence in the Philippines became more complicated. The immediate concern of the Americans was to restore and expand the Philippine economy to prevent the islands from being a burden on the U.S. treasury. Massive public works programs, such as construction of roads, ports and harbors, were undertaken. Transportation and communication networks were established. Science and technology, which during the Spanish regime was almost exclusively an activity of academia and a few individual scientists, became a major government activity. The Bureau of Science was established and soon began to receive international recognition, until its destruction during World War II. Whereas initial commercial potential of the Philippines was merely as a trading post to China and the rest of Asia, certain American interests began to see the Philippines as a potential economic colony, *i.e.,* a supplier of raw materials and consumer of American goods (Grunder and Livezey, 1951:28-29; 40-41; Wolfe, 1960:152-160).

The Americans inherited the oppressive land tenure system from the Spaniards, upon which most of the Pilipinos depended for a living. Some of the encomiendas and the friar lands were bought by the U.S. government and

---

[12] Agoncillo and Alfonso, *History of the Filipino People,* 1971:117-118.

became public lands. The Organic Act limited the acquisition of public lands for purchase or lease at 1,024 hectares for corporations and 16 hectares for individual homesteaders.[13] There was a move from certain U.S. interests to increase the size of land that could be purchased or leased to corporations and to allow foreigners (Americans) to develop them. The rationale was that cash crop agriculture could not be operated efficiently on small holdings and that there was not enough local capital to develop plantation type, mechanized agriculture. The move was opposed by Pilipino and American political leaders who feared that the move would open the way for economic exploitation of the Philippines. Some Americans in the Philippines (administrators, military commanders and those in academic and church institutions) knew that land tenure was the major socioeconomic problem, and that unless there was a change in the land tenure system, the situation would worsen, regardless of whether the Philippines became part of the U.S. or an independent nation.

The land and tenancy system was not resolved during the American administration, nor after the administration ended. The encomiendas either passed on to heirs or were sold to new landowners (families and corporations), and since they were not public lands, they were not subject to the size limitations. Some of the friar lands were subdivided and sold or leased to former tenants. But eventually, most of them ended up in the hands of the ruling elite families. Introducing an equitable land tenure system was one innovation that the Americans could have initiated for the majority of the Pilipinos since they had the political clout to carry it out. Yet they failed to do this. The intentions were there, but they were no match for the economic and political interests, both in the Philippines and the U.S., who preferred the old system. The Pilipino landowners refused to give up their economic advantages. By and large, the Americans in the U.S. were unenthusiastic about land reforms since this was an internal matter. In other words, the land tenure problem was a Pilipino problem that did not impinge on American interests, and therefore was left to the Pilipinos to resolve (Grunder and Livezey, 1951:80-82; 127-136; Corpus, 1965:33-34).

American action (or inaction) on the Philippine land tenure problem typified the American posture on its economic policies on the Philippines *vis-a-vis* the U.S. The American body politic supported and enacted measures that were to benefit the Philippines (and many did), but only as long as they did not conflict with American governmental or private economic interests. Even those actions that benefited the Philippines went only to the elite and the urban centers, and rarely filtered down to the rest of the people (Grunder and Livezey, 1951:104-121; McWilliams, 1964:246-247; Pomeroy, 1970:172-228).

Highlights and Implications of the American Experience. Regardless of American motives for the development of the Philippines, the fact remains that, compared

---

[13] Under the metric system, which is used in the Philippines, one hectare is approximately 2.4 acres.

to other Asian and African countries, the country was far more developed economically and politically at the time of its political independence from the U.S., than the Asian and African colonies were at the time of their own independence. For instance, at the end of the American administration, all governmental structures were in the hands of Pilipinos. Most of the supervisory level, some decision making and all lower level positions in American business and industry were occupied by Pilipinos. Compared with three centuries of Spanish colonization, the half century of formal dominance and colonial rule of America was more thorough and effective. Technological advances in the communications media also had a significant contribution towards the Americanization of the Philippines. The spread of the written media and radio (particularly the transistor radio) allowed the dissemination of information and ideas even in geographically isolated areas of the country. Also through the same media, information and ideas critical of the U.S. were disseminated, whereas they had been previously confined to high level political and academic circles.

It has often been said that where Spanish arms failed, Spanish religion succeeded, thus the Philippines was conquered by the cross rather than the sword. One can therefore draw the same conclusion about American presence and domination of Philippine life. Where American gunboats failed, the American educational system, advertising and the soft-sell approach succeeded in seducing at least a generation of Pilipinos to the "American way", if not by choice at least by perceived necessity. As late as 1970, a group was organized in the Philippines whose aim was to have the country returned to the United States to eventually become a state. The movement never acquired significance in the Philippines, much less in the U.S., but it was reported to have been able to recruit six million members, supporters and even financial contributors (*Newsweek.* July 24, 1972:50-51).

An Interlude: World War II and Postwar Era. There were some speculations that, had the Philippines not been a colony of the U.S. or had been an independent nation, it would not have been included in the Japanese War agenda. From hindsight, it can be hypothesized that this could not have made a difference. Thailand was a neutral country and it was not spared being used by the Japanese. Japan's message to Asian countries was of their intention to liberate them from their white colonial masters. Like some Indonesians, Malaysians and Indochinese, there may have been some Pilipinos who entertained such hopes. The Japanese sponsored a "republic" replete with flying the Philippine flag (replacing the Japanese rising sun), a civil government and even a constabulary under the eyes and ears of Japanese "advisers" and their collaborators. However, Pilipino suppporters were soon shattered by Japanese destruction, atrocities and oppression. The Japanese, contrary to their propaganda, came as conquerors rather than liberators.

The highly publicized retreat to the island bastion of Corregidor, the last stand at Bataan, followed by the notorious death march at which thousands of American and Pilipino prisoners of war perished, cemented American-Pilipino relations (at least at the emotional level) further. There followed years of guerrilla-type warfare initially conducted by almost independent warlords, each claiming to be the legitimate guerrilla movement. Later, American and Pilipino officers and civilian officials came to the islands and unified the movement with direct radio links and supplies from Australia. Buoyed by Gen. Douglas MacArthur's "I shall return" battle cry and by the fact that the Philippines was to get its independence in 1946, according to the 1934 Tydings-McDuffie Act, the Pilipinos resisted and fought the Japanese until the latter were defeated in 1945 (Agoncillo and Alfonso, 1967:453-525).

The guerilla movement spawned a nationalist-agrarian movement led by the Communist and Socialist parties, who saw an opportunity to carry out agrarian, social, economic and political reforms after the Japanese were defeated. Although they carried their share of the fighting in the war and were able to get representatives elected to Congress in 1946, they were outlawed and deprived of their congressional seats by the new republic at the insistence of American "advisers" and "consultants". Thus, those who fought the Japanese were now haunted by former Japanese collaborators who got full support from the Americans. They became known by their war time name of "Hublahaps" or "Huks" and fought government forces intermittently until the 1960s. The split between the Soviet Union and China and between the "Stalinists" and "Maoists" also affected the movement. However, their struggle for social and economic reforms or at least political participation has continued to this day, exacerbated by the Marcos martial law regime. No longer called Huks, but NPA (New People's Army), it has expanded beyond just being a peasant movement, with leadership and following from urban dwellers, middle class, professionals, workers and students (Agoncillo and Alfonso, 1967:525-547; Shalom, 1981).

Continued Dominance of the United States. Formal independence in 1946 did not end American domination of the Philippines. For instance, immediately after independence was granted, the Philippine Constitution was amended to allow American citizens the same rights as Pilipinos in the exploitation of natural resources and the operation of certain businesses, such as retail trade and utilities. Succeeding agreements and treaties retained and expanded American domination of the Philippines, although the language of the treaties and political rhetoric gave them a nationalistic flavor. U.S. foreign "aid" to the Philippines, starting with the Philippine Rehabilitation Act by the U.S. Congress, was tailored to suit U.S. economic and political interests, rather than Philippine needs. (Grunder and Livezey, 1951:248-275; McWilliams, 1964:245-248; Diokno, 1968:11-19; Pomeroy, 1974; Shalom, 1981). Some of the more blatant statutes such as the retail trade and public utilities privileges for U.S. citizens were later abrogated by the courts, a decision sustained by the Philippine Supreme Court.

Another example of U.S. dominance is the continued existence of U.S. military installations in the Philippines, principally, Clark in Pampanga, headquarters of the U.S. 13th Air Force Command, and the naval base in Subic Bay, Zambales.[14] The existence of a foreign military establishment in a

---

[14] Clark Air Base in Pampanga, the U.S. naval base in Subic Bay and the Cubi Air Station in Zambales are the largest U.S. military installations in the Philippines involving several thousand

country does not necessarily mean domination of one over the other, provided they are covered by regional agreements such as the North Atlantic Treaty Organization (NATO), and provided further that the agreements show some recognition of the sovereignty and national sensibilities of the host nation.

However, the 1947 Philippine-United States agreement governing the presence of U.S. military bases in the Philippines was something else. First, the agreement was supposed to last for 99 years at no cost to the U.S. except for U.S. military assistance. Second, the U.S. had almost absolute extraterritorial (*i.e.,* military, political, economic and judicial) jurisdiction over the bases. U.S. personnel outside the bases were protected by Philippine laws, and their offenses were likewise subject to the Philippine judicial system. Base authorities were supposed to turn over offending U.S. personnel to Philippine authorities. Offenses committed by U.S. personnel within the base, including those against Pilipinos, were subjected to U.S. military courts (U.S. Department of State, 1948). However, more often than not, U.S. personnel accused of offenses outside the bases or committed against Pilipinos inside or along the base perimeters were sent out of the country before their cases could be adjudicated either by the U.S. or Philippine authorities. A constant irritant was the wounding or killing by U.S. security guards of Pilipinos for alleged pilfering.

Moreover, as past and recent history has shown, the U.S. military presence in the Philippines is primarily there for U.S. interests, as well as for providing tactical support for U.S. military intervention in Asia, Middle East and the Indian Ocean area. So far, there is no evidence that the U.S. has permanent hardened silos in the Philippines for heavy multi-warhead strategic nuclear missiles. However, its known that they do store tactical nuclear weapons as part of the forward strike bases for a U.S. air and seaborne nuclear first strike capability (Schrimer, 1982; Hutchcroft, 1982; Church Coalition for Human Rights in the Philippines, n.d.). Hence, as early as the 1940s, in addition to nationalist sentiments, opposition to the U.S. bases in the Philippines was based on the fact that should the U.S. become involved in a major (and nuclear) war, the Philippines will be (and are in fact) targets of the Soviet Union and other countries at war with the U.S. This would subject the Philippines to a nuclear war and other military actions, for which they have little or no say, nothing to gain and everything to lose (Recto and Constantino, n.d.; Emmanuel, 1983).

Local, provincial (and some national) officials and business leaders where the bases are located (Olongapo City, Zambales province for the Subic naval base and Angeles City, Pampanga province for Clark Airbase) have tried and continue to exert efforts to keep the bases. Not only do the bases fuel the local economies, but they directly provide about 40,000 civilian jobs to Pilipinos, not to mention peripheral employment in the "entertainment" and other businessess dependent on base personnel. However, the bases are also a

---

hectares and millions of dollars in permanent installations. However, there are at least eleven other military-related installations throughout the Philippines, ranging from the microwave communication relay station in northern Luzon to the U.S. Air Force's atomic energy detection system in Mindanao (U.S. Department of State, 1979; Berry, 1983).

source of crime and unsavory activities, from smuggling of consumer goods (which competes unfairly with legitimate business and deprives the country of duties and taxes) to illegal traffic in drugs, to prostitution, as well as major sources of illegal weapons used in crime and by political elements opposed to the government. The cost-benefit issues of this non-military aspect of the presence of U.S military bases in the Philippines has been and will continue to be confronted by affected Philippine national, provincial and local officials, for as long as they are there.

The 1979 amendment to the bases agreement was adjusted to remove some of the most objectionable provisions to the Philippines, if not in substance, at least symbolically. Among the salient features are the following: 1) the agreement is for five years, subject to renegotiation every five years; 2) the bases will be Philippine military installations which will fly the Philippine flag and will be under a Pilipino base commander, (there will be an American "base facilities commander" who will have jurisdiction over U.S. personnel and facilities); 3) criminal jurisdiction of U.S. personnel will be similar to those in U.S. military installations in NATO countries and Japan, plus, U.S. authorities will retain an offending person until an agreement is reached on the disposition of the case in cases involving official duties; 4) the Pilipino base commander and Pilipinos will provide for security (*i.e.,* Pilipinos, not Americans, will wound or kill unauthorized Pilipinos in the bases); and 5) the U.S. will, in the next five years, provide the Philippines with $500 million dollars in military assistance, military sales credits and "security supporting assistance" (U.S. Department of State, 1979).[15] These amendments not only reflect a more independent stance of the Philippines *vis-a-vis* the United States, they also reflect the geopolitical changes in the region and the world at large across time, for example, the reduction of American military presence in Asia at the end of the Vietnam War, and the opening of diplomatic relations between the Philippines and the Soviet Union and Peoples Republic of China.

The latest (1983-84) negotiations for the renewal of the bases agreement reflect the shifts in relationships between the two countries, as well as provide a dilemma to Philippine political leaders opposed to the Marcos regime and the presence of U.S bases in the country and to the U.S. body-politic. U.S. defense authorities still insist that the military installations in the Philippines are essential to the U.S., although there are some, including high-ranking U.S. retired military personnel, who claim that this is not so; that it is only convenient to have them in the Philippines as opposed to moving them to U.S. territory, such as Guam and Hawaii. The position of the U.S military provides President Marcos the leverage to demand what he wants in return for the use of the bases; which is basically $900 million for five years in rent,

[15] The author gratefully acknowledges the assistance extended by the following in securing copies and information relevant to the Philippine-United States agreements governing the U.S. military installations in the Philippines: Office of Internal Security, Politico-Military Affairs, U.S. Department of State; Embassy of the Philippines, Washington, D.C. and the Office of Senator Donald W. Reigle, Jr. (D-Michigan).

rather than in aid.

There is no agreement within the U.S. body-politic on whether this money should be in the form of rent or aid and, if in the latter how much would be for military and non-military purposes. The opposition both in the Philippines and in the U.S. would prefer to have the bases relocated. However, they realize this will not be the case in the immediate future. As nationalists, they prefer that the U.S. pay rent for the bases without any strings attached or dictation on how it should be spent. However, as oppositionists to the Marcos regime, they fear that without the checks and balances in the present Philippine government, this would be tantamount to giving the Marcos regime $900 million for five years "to play with" as it sees fit. So they grit their teeth and suggest that it be given in aid, rather than rent, and if possible all non-military aid (U.S. Congress House Committee on Foreign Affairs, 1983). At any rate, the renewal or continuance of the U.S. military bases in the Philippines, regardless of which administration is in power in both countries, will continue to be an important role in Philippine-United States relations. They will also continue to be debated among the Pilipinos in the U.S. or elsewhere.

AGRO-INDUSTRIAL EVOLUTION OF THE U.S. ECONOMY AND THE NEED FOR NON-SLAVE LABOR

Several structural changes were occurring in the United States towards the end of the 19th and the start of the 20th centuries that would eventually affect the immigration of Pilipinos to the U.S.: the changes in U.S. agriculture and its competitive position in world commerce; the abolition of slavery and the need for certain types of labor that could not be met by domestic sources; the difficulties involved in using aliens for certain types of work; and the structural linkages between the Philippines and the United States that facilitated the use of Pilipino labor in the latter, as well as the attendant domestic and transnational implications.

The Need for and Problems of Non-Slave and Immigrant Laborers

The era of reconstruction following the Civil War led to the development of the United States from an agricultural to an industrial country and a world industrial and economic power. Expanding industries in the East and North and in some areas in the Midwest were absorbing the white immigrants and some of the freed slaves, who also filled low-skilled service jobs in the urban centers. The West was expanding, particularly in mining and railroads. Most of the whites who could not be accommodated in industrial urban labor moved to the West and Midwest as farmers to try their fortunes on the frontiers. A good number of freed slaves stayed on in southern plantations as tenant sharecroppers or as independent marginal farmers.

Highly mobile unmarried male gang labor was needed to provide the low-skilled work on railroads, in mines and in service occupations in frontier towns. Chinese "coolie" labor provided the solution to this problem. However, the Chinese became "problems" when they were no longer needed and they started becoming independent entrepreneurs (McWilliams, 1964:89-101).

In the meantime, California and Hawaiian agriculture was undergoing changes. Whereas family operated farms initially provided for the agricultural needs of the nation, there was now a need for an agricultural system that would make the U.S. competitive in world markets for certain cash crops such as wheat, sugar and cattle. The operations had to be better organized and on a larger scale than the antebellum plantations in order to meet the demands of the export markets. Thus, the concept of factory type agriculture - or agribusiness - was adopted. Hawaii and California provided the initial testing grounds for this type of agricultural operation. This precipitated the forcing out of family farms and settlers, followed by the buying out of estates from some Spanish landowners, and later, through the connivance of local and state officials, the taking over of large tracts of public land by large farmers or corporations (McWilliams, 1939:11-66).

Initial labor was provided by poor mobile male whites, who became a unique American social phenomenon - "hobos" - who provided the seasonal labor. They were supplemented by Native Americans and Mexicans during and between seasons. Needless to say, the latter groups were paid less for the same work than the white hobos were. However, the Native Americans soon became unreliable, and the hobos were also becoming less available, while there was a threat of cutting off immigration from Mexico. Thus the unwanted Chinese at the railroads, mines and urban centers were readily absorbed into the agricultural "factories" of California and Hawaii. Additional Chinese immigrated to fill this need. The Chinese, followed by the Japanese and Pilipinos, turned California and Hawaii into an "oriental agriculture" in the U.S. (McWilliams, 1939:81-133).

However, the Chinese were never satisfied with being wage laborers. Before long they became independent entrepreneurs in California, thereby depriving the economy of cheap coolie labor. As more and more Chinese immigrated to the U.S., the threats they posed to the economic domination of whites became more evident and evoked chambers of horror perceptions to the chronic racists who envisioned the "yellow peril" as threats to the purity of the white race. Thus, economic and racial factors against the Chinese led to the enactment of the first U.S. Immigration Law in 1882.

U.S. Immigration Policies

In a recent report, the National Commission on Manpower Policy (NCMP) contended that, compared with other countries that have received and continue to host large numbers of immigrants (*i.e.,* Canada, Australia, Israel, etc.), the United States has never had an immigration policy, but rather policies that changed over time and with the changing demands of national and international conditions. American official and unofficial atttiudes toward immigrants ranged from attracting to barring, from being humane to being racially restrictive and exploitative. This was further exacerbated by the implementation of immigration laws which were just as inconsistent as the declared policies - and sometimes inconsistent with the spirit and letter of the laws (Harper, 1975; NCMP, 1978:9-73). There can be as many arguments for as against the lack of a long-range national immigration policy.

For instance, such a policy especially for countries with limited territories and resources, can control and select the immigrants it needs and wants over a long period, whereby immigration becomes an integrated part of a national development plan. It can also give notice to potential immigrants as to whether they can qualify as immigrants or not. A policy that is selective of ethnic, racial, religious or political origins may be discriminatory. However, any nation has the right to determine who they want to admit as immigrants for such reasons as maintaining a homogeneous population. Barring nonwhite immigrants is better than admitting them and then relegating them to second class citizenship.

Conversely, it can be argued that the absence of a long-range national policy on immigration allows the country to easily adjust to the demands of changing domestic and international situations. This is precisely what the United States has been able to do, namely, restrict immigration or permit it when certain kinds of people are needed for humane and political reasons such as accommodating refugees. This flexible immigration policy (or policies as the NCMP contends) is reflected in the patterns of immigration in numbers, types and sources of immigrants. The impact of the Immigration and Nationality Act of 1965, as amended in 1976, on the patterns of immigration in general and how it affected immigration from the Philippines will be discussed in the next chapter. However, at this point it may be mentioned that the Act as amended has shifted the source of immigrants from Europe to Asia and developing countries.

Historically, U.S. immigration policies, laws and practices toward nonwhites (or non-Anglo Saxons) had dual effects, whether intended or not. When nonwhites were needed for certain sectors of the economy, U.S. immigration laws, policies and practices were liberal. But when no longer needed, these people started demanding the same rights as Americans, and when they were perceived as competitive threats by certain segments of the white population, the laws, policies and practices became restrictive and discriminatory. These structural changes in policies and laws toward nonwhite immigrants also reflected the general disposition of the majority population. In other words, favorable or unfavorable stereotyping of the nonwhites could be turned on and off, depending on the demands of the situation. Needless to say the fate of nonwhite immigrants was no different from that of the indigenous populations (Native Americans and Hispanics) and blacks.

Prior to 1882, there was no U.S. federal immigration policy, much less any laws regulating the entry of immigrants. Anyone who could afford the fare to the U.S. was welcome. It was the threat of the "yellow peril" that precipitated the first immigration acts by the U.S. directed at excluding or limiting nonwhite immigration which continued until the middle of the 1960s.

However, the U.S. racially based immigration acts set the pattern for similar acts in the "new world". Soon after the Immigration Act of 1882, Australia, New Zealand and countries in Central and South America also enacted anti-Oriental immigration laws (McWilliams, 1964:168-169; 170-228; USDOL, 1974:6-7). The Immigration Act of 1882 may have saved U.S. civilization from the "yellow peril", but it again created labor shortages in Hawaii and California. Moreover, California agriculture was shifting from wheat, cotton and cattle to vegetable and fruit horticulture, which needed less mobile, specialized, male workers who could be counted on to return to the same fields every season. Japanese immigrants solved this problem.

The Japanese policy of isolationism was partially broken by Commodore Perry in 1854. Part of this policy of isolation was the prohibition of Japanese emigration from 1638 to 1854. In response to the sugar planters in Hawaii, the U.S. government persuaded the Japanese government to relax their restrictive emigration policies. Thus, in 1854 Japanese began immigrating to the sugar plantations of Hawaii and later to the West coast. They were initially welcomed and any stereotyping of the Japanese was generally favorable. The Exclusion Act of 1882 was interpreted as being directed at the Chinese. Moreover, the Japanese immigrants were farmers and fitted nicely into the scheme of things.

Like the Chinese, the Japanese became "problems" when they began to improve their economic status at the "expense" of the economy. They saved their money, kept to themselves and during their free time started developing marginal land nobody wanted, which they leased or "squatted on". Nobody minded since they were developing areas that were the breeding grounds of disease (*i.e.,* swamp land, etc.) and were producing for their own needs. However, soon these Orientals adopted the American ethic of hard work and competition, and their farm produce began competing with that of American farmers. Briefly, this meant that Japanese farm labor was no longer available to U.S. agriculture in Hawaii and California, and laborers were now organizing into unions.

Generating anti-Japanese feelings was not difficult, since the anti-Oriental feelings of the "yellow peril" had not really disappeared, but merely subsided. The anti-Japanese movement started with the prohibition of land ownership, cultivation and even expropriation of Japanese farms. In 1907, President Theodore Roosevelt stopped the immigration of Japanese from Mexico and Canada by an executive order. This was soon followed by the "gentlemen's agreement" between the United States and Japan whereby the latter agreed to stop the emigration of Japanese who were bound for the U.S. The Immigration Acts of 1920 and 1924 severely limited the immigration of Japanese to the U.S. (McWilliams, 1939:101-133; 1964:140-169). The exclusion of the Japanese was once again creating labor shortages in Hawaii and California. In the meantime, across the Pacific Pilipino resistance to America was pacified and a civil colonial government was on the way to being well established.

The "Little Brown Brothers" provided the solution for the agricultural labor problems of Hawaii and California and the fish canneries of Alaska.[16] Here was a people who, although from the Orient, were not exactly Orientals the way the Chinese and Japanese were (*i.e.,* "mongolian races", "yellow hordes" etc.). United States policy on the Philippines had not yet been fully crystallized and, the Philippines was still considered a territory of the U.S.-bought from Spain for $25 million. However, in case after case the courts maintained that this did not confer automatic citizenship on the Pilipinos (McWilliams, 1964:242-243).

Then, in the early 1920s, in two cases involving Japanese nationals desiring to be naturalized in the U.S., (*Ozawa v. United States* and *Toyota v. United States*) the Supreme Court stated that Pilipinos are ineligible to apply for naturalization except as specifically allowed by law: those who had been honorably discharged after three years in the U.S. armed services. Thus, until the passage of the Philippine Independence Act of 1934, Pilipinos provided a pool of cheap laborers who could not become U.S. citizens nor were technically aliens. Whereas movement (immigration and exclusion) of aliens such as the Chinese, Japanese and Mexicans involved dealing with foreign governments, the movement of Pilipinos within the United States was an internal migration issue.

Moreover, centuries of Spanish oppression and exploitation had created a large pool upon which agricultural interests in the U.S. could draw. This not only solved the agricultural labor shortages on the U.S. West Coast and Hawaii, but also relieved pressures for immediate social and economic reforms in the Philippines, a situation the Americans inherited from Spain. The Pilipinos were the most logical solution to the agricultural problems of Hawaii and California. They were, in fact, effectively used in breaking Japanese strikes in the sugar plantations of Hawaii in 1909 and 1919. (Lasker, 1931:159-168; McWilliams, 1964:186). Thus, a basis was established for the large scale entry of Pilipinos to the United States.

Pilipino immigration to Hawaii and the U.S. mainland was further facilitated through massive recruiting efforts by the sugar industry. Some of the planters even established recruiting centers in the Philippines to facilitate the immigration of Pilipinos to Hawaii. The inducements were a three-year contract with wages ranging from $2.00 to $4.00 per day, free passage to Hawaii and housing. McWilliams (1964:234-236) contends that the massive and often deceptive recruiting of Pilipino laborers created a pull rather than a push factor. However, there is some doubt as to whether the attractiveness of the recruitment efforts was solely responsible for the immigration. Undoubtedly, as the "Americanization" of the Pilipinos began to take effect, the U.S. became more attractive.

There is evidence to indicate that other forces were also operating to encourage Pilipino immigration. By the middle of the 1920s, it was no longer necessary for the recruiters to offer passage money. Potential immigrants were not only willing to pay the passage themselves, but even to give more

---

[16] The term is lifted from the title of a book by Leon Wolfe, *Little Brown Brothers*, which describes the United States takeover of the Philippines from Spain in 1898. It was originally published by Doubleday and Company, Inc., in 1960, and has been republished by Erehwon Press, Manila, 1971.

money to the recruiters to assure their being chosen as immigrants from among the many applicants. Many applicants with some education tried to pass themselves off as illiterates, since it was alleged that recruiters for the Hawaiian plantations were only hiring illiterates, on the belief that they would more likely remain on the plantations and do the work for which they were recruited and contracted (Alcantara, 1981:35; Teodoro, Jr., 1981).

Most of the immigrants came from economically depressed areas, from sectors of the Philippines where the tenancy system predominated and from the urban proletariat. Except for some students and a few semi-skilled blue and white collar workers, the immigrants were mostly of rural and peasant origins with little or no formal education (Lasker, 1931:145-147; 230; 237-241). In other words, there were more potential immigrants than were needed in Hawaii and California. In addition to being bilked by recruiters in order to be included as immigrants, they were overcharged for their fares and for the "preparation of travel papers". The agricultural interests of Hawaii and California got their cheap source of labor while the recruiters, travel agencies and steamship companies made more money, all at the expense of the Pilipino immigrants (Lasker, 1931:203-217; Catapusan, 1940:11-24; McWilliams, 1964:234-236).

Structural Implications for Immigration

The major concerns of the average Pilipino at the turn of the century were economic security (mostly through land reform), educational opportunities for themselves and their children, social justice and political independence. The inequities of the tenancy system which kept them perpetually in debt did not provide any hope in the foreseeable future. Some attempted to supplement their income by wage employment during off-seasons or by sending members of the family to urban centers for low-wage labor or as domestic servants, all of which were to no avail.

The short-lived Republic at the end of Spanish colonization was followed by almost four years of conventional and later guerrilla type warfare against the Americans. The end of the war and re-establishment of a civil government in which Pilipino participation was maximized provided political stability. However, the pre-American agrarian unrest and economic deprivation persisted. The Spanish *encomiendas* were formally abolished, but the same oppressive and exploitative system continued under a new name, the *hacienda* or plantation type agriculture, this time under the native elites in collaboration with American business interests.

There was a marked improvement in the overall economy of the country in terms of new infrastructures and increased revenues from international trade. However, these were mostly confined to the metropolis and the beneficiaries were mainly the elites and a middle class growing from commerce and expanding bureaucracies. The majority who lived on the land continued to be economically deprived and many migrated to urban centers, thus adding to the large number of unemployed and underemployed unskilled in the labor force.

The taking over of the Philippines by the United States provided the linkages that precipitated the immigration of a large Pilipino pool of surplus labor that had been building. The emigration of large numbers of Pilipinos from economically depressed areas, sectors where the mode of agriculture was under the tenancy (hacienda) system, and from the urban proletariat helped relieve some of the pressures on the Philippine body-politic and leadership, thus curtailing action or immediate and drastic agrarian economic reforms.

By the 1930s, the Pilipino leadership began to be concerned about the emigration of Pilipinos to the U.S. Although the term "brain drain" had not yet been conceived, Philippine authorities were already concerned with the drain of the "youth of the land" as well as the semi-skilled industrial workers (Lasker, 1931:273-283). Moreover, they were also concerned with the discrimination and hostilities the Pilipinos were encountering in the U.S. Some of the agrarian pressure was relieved when new lands were opened on the island of Mindanao, where former tenant sharecroppers were given their own homesteads. Unfortunately, this was the era before agricultural extension, rural credit and all the support that small farmers need in a modern economy. A good number of would-be landowners had to abandon their homesteads, drifting to urban areas to join a growing army of proletariat or becoming sharecroppers again.

In the meantime, a large number of new generation Pilipinos were getting an American education. This resulted in higher or different life expectations. Many no longer wanted to make a living on the land as their parents did, even if the land were made available. This was compounded by the fact that the land never did become available, as the old land tenure system continued to prevail. The new generation of Pilipinos also had different lifestyle expectations, becoming consumer oriented towards American products, while at the same time the national economy was not developing fast enough to allow satisfaction of real and perceived needs. The only way to live like Americans was to be in America. Thus, immigration continued to persist until 1940, although the actual flow of immigrants was restricted in 1935 by U.S. immigration laws. The economic and political dislocation brought about by World War II only exacerbated the situation.

Philippine political independence in 1946 did not change the situation much. Land tenure continued to be a problem and the best perceived way of getting a better living was getting out of the land or going into an occupation which could only be done with an education. Thus, the Philippines underwent an "educational boom" in the decades following World War II. By the 1960s, the Philippines had the second highest number of college students at 1,560 per 100,000 of the population and was exceeded only by the U.S. at 2,840 per 100,000 of its population (UNESCO, 1968). The Philippine economy was showing some "improvement" in terms of gross national product (GNP) type statistics. However, for the rest of the people, especially the growing army of college trained, the situation was getting worse. Once again, emigration was perceived as a way out, only this time it was for a large pool of "educated proletariat" that had been building up during the decades following World War II.

SUMMARY

The national, international and Philippine-U.S. structures that precipitated the immigration of Pilipinos to the U.S. may be summarized as follows. First, centuries of Spanish colonial rule followed by years of war for independence deprived rural and urban labor surplus in the Philippines. Secondly, U.S. agriculture, in order to maintain its competitiveness in world commerce, was changing from family size farms and slave labor plantations to large scale agricultural/horticultural "factories" or agribusinesses, particularly in Hawaii and the U.S. West Coast, which precipitated the need for cheap, nonslave labor for certain types of agricultural work. Finally, the acquisition of the Philippines by the U.S., whereby the Philippines became a territory or "ward" of the latter, provided the political, economic and social linkages that allowed the "internal" and "voluntary" migration of Pilipino labor to U.S. territories and the mainland without the domestic and diplomatic difficulties associated with the immigration of other alien workers such as the Chinese, Japanese and Mexicans.

The next chapter will examine how these structural changes across time and space precipitated Pilipino immigration to the United States and affected the type of immigrants, patterns of immigration and integration of the immigrants.

4. The "Little Brown Brothers" Discover America

PATTERNS OF PILIPINO IMMIGRATION TO THE UNITED STATES

As noted earlier, the Philippines and the Pilipinos were not brought to the American public's attention until the late 1880s when the United States acquired the country from Spain. There was very little, if any, documentation on Pilipinos in the U.S., official or otherwise. However, long before this period, Pilipinos (students, intellectual and economic elites and some political exiles) had been traveling outside the Philippines, mostly to Europe (mainly to Spain) and Asia. Some may have included the U.S. in their itineraries, and may have even stayed for periods of time, but not as immigrants. Nonetheless, a little known fact is that Pilipino seamen lived along the Louisiana coast (and there was even a "Manila Village" in Jefferson Parish) as early as the middle of the 1700s. It may be noted, however, that at this time Louisiana was not yet part of the United States (Espina, 1974:117-221). It was not until the beginning of this century, especially in the 1920s, that the Philippine and U.S. governments started taking more interest and systematically documenting the movement of Pilipinos in and out of the U.S. Hence, most reliable information about Pilipinos in the U.S. dates back only to this period.

McWilliams reports that the first Pilipinos to come to the U.S. before 1920 were students. They were easily accepted by the academic communities, since many of them were sponsored by missionary related educational institutions and the U.S. government. Most came from the middle to upper socioeconomic classes. They became showcases of how Americans treated their new wards in the Pacific. Of course, it was then chic to have Pilipino houseboys (students paying for their own education). Labor recruitment, initially for Hawaii, later spilled over to the mainland. By the 1920s more laborers were directly recruited to the mainland or went there on their own, particularly after the passage of the Immigration Acts of 1920 and 1924, which barred the immigration of Japanese. Thus, according to McWilliams, between 1907 and 1930 an estimated 150,000 Pilipinos emigrated, of whom fewer than half were on the U.S. mainland and the rest in Hawaii (McWilliams, 1964:234-235).

The first major recruiting of Pilipino labor for Hawaii and the U.S. occurred between 1905 and 1929 (Lasker, 1931:3-6; Catapusan, 1940:11-17). By 1929 the estimated Pilipino population in the U.S. was 80,000. By 1940 there were 125,000 Pilipinos in the U.S., and by 1960 there were 176,000 (Morales, 1974:70). Not all Pilipinos in the U.S. came as laborers; a minority were students supported by the U.S. government or church related/missionary groups, some of whom elected to stay after their studies. Prior to 1935, there were no limitations on the number of Pilipinos moving in or out of U.S. territories, since they were not considered aliens. In fact, Pilipinos leaving the Philippines were issued U.S. passports.

The peculiar or "special" relations between the Philippines and the U.S. had its repercussions in the U.S., particularly on the Pilipino residents on the mainland or in U.S. territories. Unlike other nonwhite foreigners who were also brought to the U.S., the Pilipinos were not considered aliens but "nationals". Consequently, they could not be deported or excluded from U.S. territory whenever and wherever they became "problems". To have done so would not only have violated the then existing U.S. laws, but would have also been inconsistent with the policy of keeping the Philippines a colony (Lasker, 1931; McWilliams, 1939 and 1942; Catapusan, 1940:74; and 82-89; Konvits, 1946:101-106; Mathews, 1970:268-284). It was argued that exclusion of Pilipinos from the U.S. was the price they had to pay for independence. One of the strongest supporters for Philippine independence was U.S. organized labor, since this was the U.S. labor force (Lasker, 1931:298-317; Grunder and Levezey, 1951:195-219).

In July of 1935, President Franklin D. Roosevelt signed into law the Welch Bill (H.R. 6464) which appropriated $300,000 to pay the fare of Pilipinos who voluntarily returned to the Philippines. Very few took advantage of this. Among the reasons for its failure was that by 1936 the economic situation in the U.S. had improved, allowed for more and better jobs for the would-be repatriates; Pilipino leaders both in the U.S. and the Philippines saw it as an insult to the Pilipinos and a back-handed way of getting them out of the U.S. Another reason was that Pilipinos who accepted some form of aid from the government were ostracized by their own people both in the U.S. and in the Philippines. There was some apprehension on the part of the potential repatriates that although the repatriation was voluntary, the fact that it was not paid for by the repatriate might be perceived as a failure of the person's sojourn in the U.S (*i.e.,* the person did not become and return rich); or the stigma of deportation was associated with a government paid ticket home (Bogardus, 1936:67-71; Catapusan, 1936:72-77).

In 1935, when the Philippines was granted commonwealth status prior to "full independence" in 1946, the entry of Pilipinos to the U.S. as immigrants was limited to fifty persons per year, following a quota system based on national origins, pursuant to the existing immigration statutes. At the time of independence in 1946, the quota of allowable Pilipino immigrants to the U.S. was increased to 100 per year. These included only Pilipinos admitted as immigrants directly from the Philippines. Special laws and bilateral agreements between the Philippines and the U.S. governed the status of Pilipinos already in the U.S. in 1935 and 1946 (Grunder and Levezey, 1951:205; 261-264). This system remained in force until the promulgation of the U.S. Immigration and Nationality Act of 1965.

The chronology of Pilipino immigration to the U.S. may be summarized by several periods related to various stages of Philippine-U.S. relations: 1905-1935 when there was unlimited immigration; 1935 to 1940 when the number was limited to fifty persons per year; 1940 to 1946, during World War II, when there was a suspension of direct immigration but during which a number of Pilipinos in the U.S. Armed Services and those stranded in the U.S. were later granted immigrant status; 1946 to 1964 when the number of immigrants from the Philippines was increased from fifty to a hundred persons per year; and 1965 to the present, during which Pilipino immigration was governed by the Immigration and Nationality Act of 1965.[17]

However, in terms of numbers and types of Pilipino immigrants admitted to the U.S., the most significant periods were those between 1905 and 1935, and 1965 and the present. The number of immigrants between 1936 and 1965 were too few to have a significant impact on either the Philippines or the U.S. For purposes of this study, the Pilipinos that immigrated to the U.S. between 1905 and 1964 will be referred to as the early Pilipino immigrants or simply early immigrants, and those who came after 1965 will be referred to as the new Pilipino immigrants or simply new immigrants.[18]

The Early Pilipino Immigrants: Characteristics and Behavioral Profile

The contract workers bound for Hawaii were usually met at the docks by labor contractors or employers and brought to their place of employment (plantations). However, most of the Pilipinos who came to the U.S. mainland did not have such a preimmigration network. The *modus operandi* was to establish preimmigration networks in the U.S. with relatives, friends or townmates that preceded the would-be immigrants. The latter not only

---

[17] Section 329 and its interpretation of the Immigration and Nationality Act as amended allowed Pilipino citizens who served in the U.S. Armed Forces in World War II to immigrate to the U.S. if they wished. However, few veterans took advantage of this. Syndicated columnist Jack Anderson, as late as 1978, reported that the U.S. Justice Department was making it difficult for Pilipinos to take advantage of this Law (even those already in the U.S.), notwithstanding a court ruling to the contrary (Anderson, December 6, 1978:A-8). *See also*, the 1953 Immigration and Nationality Act (Public Law 84-414).

[18] These terms should not be confused with similar terms used in the American literature describing immigration to the U.S. The latter's "old immigrants" referred to those of Anglo Saxon origins that immigrated to the U.S. from the first settlers on the Mayflower to the end of the 19th century. The "new immigrants" refer to the immigrants that came to the U.S. from Southern, Eastern and Mediterranean Europe and Ireland towards the end of the 19th and beginning of the 20th centuries.

met the immigrants at the docks in San Francisco, but also provided the initial residence, money (gifts or loans) and, in general, tips on how to get along in the system. In most instances, they also provided the first links to jobs.

McWilliams aptly describes the fate of those who did not have such preimmigration networks.

> Pilipino immigrants were caught in a weird California whirligig from the moment of their arrival in San Francisco. For years, fly-by-night taxi drivers transported newly arrived Filipinos from the Embarcadero to Stockton - one of the large Filipino concentrations. The taxi fare for a group of four or five Filipinos would be around $65 or $75, while the regular train or bus fare would have been about $2.00 per person. Taxi drivers, rooming-house operators, labor agents, and Filipino contractors - all were on the lookout for the "Pinoy" as they arrived in San Francisco full of curiosity about the land of Daniel Webster, Abraham Lincoln and William Howard Taft. (1964:236-237).

Pilipino immigrants returning to the Philippines, either for a visit or permanently who did not have relatives or friends meet them at the docks, and later at the Manila International Airport, met the same fate. They had a reception committee composed of taxi and *colorom* drivers (private cars for hire), pimps and all types of shysters, who for fees offered to help them clear customs and have a "good time" in Manila before driving them or putting them on the boat or plane to their towns and homes.

Except for a few students and government (civil and military) personnel training in the U.S., most of the early immigrants were those that were recruited as cheap contract labor. The majority were unschooled, unskilled and came from rural and lower socioeconomic status (SES) in the Philippines. Most were employed in low-skilled agricultural labor ("stoop work"), the same kind of work they left in the Philippines. Between the agricultural seasons or when work was unobtainable on the farms, they would go to the fishing canneries of Alaska (which was also seasonal and coincided with the off-season in agriculture) or obtain jobs in low-wage service work in the cities (waiters, busboys, domestic help) (Lasker, 1931:33-91; Catapusan, 1940: 25-26). Those employed in cities were generally better off than the farm workers. For a while, 4,000 were employed in the merchant marine. However, a 1937 law requiring that the crew of U.S. flag vessels be at least 90 percent American citizens closed this source of employment. Of the more than 100,000 Pilipinos in the U.S. in 1930, only 635 were classified as being in "general trade". One rather ususual case was a Pilipino inventor who set up a shop in New York employing several dozen Pilipinos and Americans (Lasker, 1931:83; 136; McWilliams, 1964:236-237).

Like most nonwhite minorities, Pilipinos were stereotyped and channeled into certain kinds of work. In urban employment, it was the service and culinary occupations. In agriculture, they were perceived as suitable for harvesting asparagus, lettuce, carrots and sugar beets. It was the common belief that the Pilipinos were not bothered by the peat dust in which asparagus grew, and that since they were smaller, they could stoop more easily than bigger or taller workers, hence their suitability for "stoop labor" (McWilliams, 1964:239-240). However, upon closer examination of the type of the crops and operations involved, it was found that they were

> ...the type in which family labor cannot be utilized; children and women can pick peaches, apricots, and cherries, but they cannot cut asparagus. To cut asparagus, an army of single men is needed and, for greater efficiency, this army must be tied to the cutting of asparagus so that it will return year after year to the same work. Denied other types of work by prejudice, and always in debt to the Filipino labor contractor - usually for a gambling debt - the single Filipino makes the ideal asparagus cutter precisely because he can be, and is, ostracized. The basis of this ostracism is really not racial or cultural or social; it is economic. Instead of saying that Filipinos are set apart because they are "different", it would be more accurate to say that they are regarded as different because they cut asparagus. Actually, "asparagus" has more to do with their status than "race" or "culture". (McWilliams, 1964:240).

Often practiced was the tactic of allocating certain types of farm labor or locations to various ethnic groups. For a long while this proved effective in making them compete with each other, thereby retarding any unification of all agricultural workers regardless of their race or ethnicity. When occasions warranted, one ethnic group was used to break the unionization movements and work stoppages or strikes of another (Jamieson, 1945). However, there were instances where the Pilipinos were able to secure some gains through organized action.

Another factor that retarded the Pilipinos' efforts at improving their working conditions was that they were not hired directly by the planters but by labor contractors, many of whom were Pilipinos who were also their gang or straw bosses. Technically, therefore, grievances were directed at the contractors rather than the planters. The Pilipino workers' relationships with the Pilipino contractor, gang or straw boss made it difficult for the former to demand better working conditions. First of all, the contractors determined who could or could not be hired or fired. Secondly, the laborers were more often than not in financial or social debt to the contractors who provided them with the jobs and loans, mostly to pay gambling debts (Lasker, 1931:85-91; McWilliams, 1964:240). Last but not least was the fact that the one group that could have helped them the most, U.S. organized labor, was one of the groups that opposed immigration and espoused exclusion of Pilipino labor from the U.S.

Initially, the Pilipino immigrants thought that the major barrier to getting better jobs was their low educational background and skills. In due time they began to realize that their inability to secure better employment or treatment from employers were only manifestations of the status they had in the larger society. This was manifested in the similarity of the patterns by which they were treated with those of the other nonwhite minorities. Among the most blatant were: getting paid lower wages than whites doing the same work; being jumped over in employment or promotions by whites who had lower qualifications or seniority; and being rejected in employment when they had the qualifications that the jobs required (Lasker, 1931:81-84; Catapusan, 1940:29; McWilliams, 1964:240-241; Bulusan, 1946; Buaken, 1948).

One of the most acute sociopsychological problems that early immigrants had to confront was the separation from their families. Less than one third of the Pilipino population were women. Most of the immigrants were single males who were either bachelors or married but did not bring their families with them, since they intended to stay only long enough to earn money to start a new life back in the Philippines (Lasker, 1931:94-95; 117; Catapusan, 1940:68-70).

Years of American tutelage in the American ideals of equality and their perceptions of the "special" relations between the Philippines and the U.S., aggravated by the rosy propaganda of labor recruiters, made them believe that they would be treated as equals by the majority, or at least better than the blacks and other minorities. Claiming equal status with whites only intensified the hostile feelings against them since they did not "know their proper places" in American society (Bogardus, 1939:59-69; 1929:469-479). The Pilipinos who attempted to marry "decent" white women became *cause célèbres,* since this was perceived as a violation of antimiscegenation laws.

Interestingly enough, their insistence on the right to marry white women was racially based. The issues involved were not the right of Pilipinos as persons to marry, but that their racial stock (Malay) made them different (and presumably better) from those covered by the antimiscegination laws, *i.e.,* the negroid or mongoloid races. When the courts upheld this contention, the California legislature quickly amended its antimiscegenation laws to include "members of the Malay race" (Lasker, 1931:169-197; Bogardus, 1931-32: 274-279; Foster, 1931-32:441-454; Kitano, 1974:234-235).

The early immigrants had very little contact with blacks, and Native Americans, principally because there were few blacks and Native Americans where there were large concentrations of Pilipinos. Their contacts with the Chinese and Japanese were hardly friendly, consisting of competition for jobs and as customers at bars, dance halls, pool halls and "recreation centers", most of which were fronts for gambling and operated by either the Chinese or Japanese. In addition to this, Pilipinos already had a preimmigration prejudice against the Chinese. The only nonwhite groups with whom the Pilipinos had substantial contacts were the Mexicans, in spite of the fact that they, too, were competitors in the labor market.

The Pilipinos and Mexicans seemed to have some racial and social affinity. Both came from rural, lower class backgrounds and were Roman Catholics who observed similar religious and social traditions derived from a common Spanish cultural heritage. The Mexicans were the only racial groups with whom many Pilipinos intermarried. There was also a belief that being Catholics, having similar racial stock and social backgrounds, Mexican wives would be more acceptable to their families in the Philippines (Catapusan, 1940:76-88).

In effect, the early Pilipino immigrants became socially and psychologically isolated in an alien environment - a situation which could have negative effects on almost anyone - but for the Pilipino, who was conditioned to confront the world as a member of a group, the experience must have been psychologically and emotionally devastating.

Initially, they were sustained emotionally by the expectation of returning home. With time, they realized that the same prejudice and discrimination that prevented integration with American society also prevented them from earning enough money to return to the Philippines. Ethnic pride as well as fear of going home without having achieved the purpose for which they had left prevented many from returning, even at the expense of the U.S. government.

The social life of the Pilipinos on the plantations consisted of playing cards, exchanging stories and singing after the work day. Few had any transportation to get to the towns. Most could not afford or did not know enough English to have a night or weekend in town. However, on a few occasions, such as between seasons, some managed to go to urban areas where Pilipinos were known to congregate, and like the urban Pilipinos, they found themselves discriminated against when pursuing some social life.

They were barred from most good restaurants, hotels, bars, etc., except in some eastern and midwestern urban centers such as New York City, Washington, D.C. or Chicago (except for rich tourists, students or officials, most Pilipinos could not afford to patronize such places anyway). Their eagerness to develop acquaintances with women gave them a reputation for being women chasers, a charge that sent the racists into hysterics. About the only "decent" social life they had was through social centers, clubs and lodges, some of which were church sponsored such as the YMCA.

For their physical, social and psychological survival, the Pilipinos resorted to cheap, exploitative commercialized entertainment. In addition to the Pilipino based lodges and social clubs, the only other social life the Pilipinos had by way of urban entertainment was in pool or dance halls and gambling. Dance hall women and prostitutes were the only white women most Pilipinos could interact with, without causing racial hostilities. The usual charge at the dance halls was ten cents for one minute of dancing, which could accumulate to a tidy sum for an evening. Pilipinos also acquired a reputation for gambling, and the pool table became a cultural artifact associated with Pilipinos. At the first official Pilipino Convention in America in 1937, it was reported that the amount derived from gambling and prostitution was estimated at two million dollars a year, which was a large sum considering that it came from the small earnings of fewer than one hundred thousand Pilipinos (Lasker, 1931:131-141; Catapusan, 1940:72-76; McWilliams, 1964:238-239).

One other way by which the early immigrants managed to survive was through Pilipino organizations, which ranged from lodges and social clubs to economic or politically oriented groups such as farm labor unions. This was surprising since the use of groups to fulfill needs and achieve goals was a cultural trait the Pilipinos brought with them. A common complaint against the farm laborers was that, compared with the Chinese, Japanese and Mexicans, the Pilipinos were quick to organize, make "unreasonable" demands, and threaten or actually walk out of their jobs at the most inopportune times, *i.e.*, during harvests (Bogardus, 1929:59-69). Compared to other nonwhite minorities, they were among those who have had the longest experience in the use of groups and group power to achieve goals. Why then have Pilipino organizations had such little impact on improving their situations?

Part of the problem was that they had no political participation and therfore could not deliver votes. Another was that any attempts to organize on a large scale for motives other than social were immediately perceived as threats by the white majority and efforts were exerted to stop or minimize their effects (Gonzalo, 1929:116-173; Mariano, 1933:66-71; Rojo, 1937:447-457; Catapusan, 1940:541-549). In addition, most of the early immigrants did not have the education enabling them to use organizations effectively in a modern industrial society.

Exacerbating the structural problems that hampered the effectiveness of Pilipino organizations was their cultural trait of organizational and group behavior - namely, the "barangay syndrome". Any Pilipino organization or interorganizational activity, be it a Bible study group, lodge, social club or labor group, was racked with factional rivalries and power conflicts. The prevalent factional conflicts often led to two negative results: first, it diluted their effectiveness in pursuing organizational goals, since the organizations' energies and resources were expended in resolving internal conflicts; and second, they precipitated in the splitting and creation of duplicate organizations pursuing the same goals but in rivalry or conflict with each other. Moreover, this Pilipino organizational trait was carried over to their interracial and interorganizational relations with the rest of the population, creating an unfavorable image of Pilipinos in other interracial organizations and of the Pilipino nation as a whole (Bogardus, 1929:59-69; McWilliams, 1964: 188-189).

Nevertheless, under intense pressure from an alien environment or when working conditions became intolerable, they managed to set aside the intra- and interorganizational rivalries and put up a united front. This was manifested at the rallies and protests against the mob violence directed against them, the bombing of Pilipino properties and police brutality (Lasker, 1931:358-368). Pilipinos were likewise successful in creating work stoppages and walkouts in California and Hawaii (McWilliams, 1939:211-229; 1964:187-189). No sooner were the movements successful, than the factional rivalries resumed, diluting any sustained action that the movements could have pursued.

Other Experiences of Early Pilipino Immigrants

McWilliams (1964:241) contends that the seasonal and geographical mobility of the Pilipinos, except those on long-term agricultural contracts, prevented the development of permanent Pilipino settlements such as "Chinatowns" and "little Tokyos". The so-called "little Manilas" in San Francisco and Los Angeles were, in fact, nothing more than "service centers" similar to the "porter towns" along the major rail lines, where Pilipinos congregated between jobs or when they were in the town. There were few Pilipino homes. Most lived in rooming houses owned by Pilipinos, Chinese or Japanese. Thus the

Pilipino "community" in the U.S. was more a blood or racial brotherhood or community of consciousness, rather than a geographical ghetto.

Another adjustment problem the early immigrants had was the disparity between their preimmigration perceptions of the U.S. and the actual situations they confronted. In addition to official U.S. propaganda and allurements of labor recruiters, a source of information which could have provided a more realistic appraisal was often misleading - the Pilipinos who were already in the United States. In their letters home they mentioned only the good things happening to them and their successes, aware that their families and friends in the Philippines had the same misconception of racial barriers as they had before coming to the U.S. The prevalence of racism in the U.S. was widely discussed and debated in the press and in political and academic circles, but this did not filter back to the rural towns and villages from which most of the immigrants came (Anthony, 1931:150-156).

The immigrants were therefore apprehensive that if they told their folks at home they could not get better paying jobs (and therefore could not send any or as much money as they should), they might not be believed, but instead it might be interpreted as an excuse for individual shortcomings, such as laziness or, worse, for squandering their earnings on "good times" (Bogardus, 1929:469-479; Gonzalo, 1929:116-173; Rojo, 1940:541-549; Burma, 1951:42-48). Sending money back was one of the main concerns of the immigrants since it was the major reason for having gone to the U.S. Many did manage to send money either on a regular basis or from time to time, but only at great personal deprivation (Lasker, 1931:251-254). One of the later works on Pilipino immigration to the U.S. by Royal F. Morales (1974) aptly describes the experience of the early immigrants to the U.S. The title of the book is *Makibaka,* meaning struggle.

The early Pilipino immigrants were also ill-informed of the changes that were happening in the Philippines during their absence. Other than news about their families and village gossip (through letters from home) the only other possible source of news available in the U.S. mainly covered problems of Pilipinos in the U.S. and the Philippine independence movement. When some of the immigrants returned to the Philippines (permanently or on visits) after a decade or more, they experienced a "reverse culture shock" upon discovering an environment that was socially, economically, politically and culturally different from the one they had left.

THE NEW PILIPINO IMMIGRANTS

Implications of the Immigration and Naturalization Act of 1965

A study sponsored by the U.S. Department of Labor (USDOL) in 1974 reported that the 1965 Immigration and Naturalization Act had been designed to meet three goals: to facilitate the unification of families; to allow admission of workers needed by the economy; and to permit the entry of a limited number of carefully defined refugees (USDOL, 1974:1).Theoretically, the racial origin quotas have been replaced by quotas from the Western and Eastern Hemispheres. The quota from the Western Hemisphere is 120,000 per year and the Eastern Hemisphere is 170,000. No one nation in the Eastern Hemisphere is allowed more than 20,000 immigrants per year. However, since the Eastern Hemisphere immigrants are also admitted under the "preference" system, actual immigrants often exceed the 170,000 quota and certain nations such as the Philippines often exceed the 20,000 national quota per year.

Another reason for the excesses is that in addition to national quotas of 20,000, there are also quotas under each preference system. The "preference" system is a set of criteria by which immigrants from the Eastern Hemisphere are allowed to enter the U.S. as immigrants in consonance with the three 1965 immigration policy goals noted.[19] Basically, they are: First Preference - unmarried adult children of U.S. citizens; Second Preference - spouses, unmarried adult children of resident aliens and their children; Third Preference - immigrants in the professions, their spouses and their children; Fourth Preference - married children of U.S. citizens, their spouses and children; Fifth Preference - siblings of U.S. citizens, their spouses and children; Sixth Preference - skilled workers, their spouses and children; Seventh Preference - refugees, their spouses and children, and an eighth category called Non-Preference - a catch-all category for those not covered by the seven preferences. The Immigration Act also places quotas of immigrants that could be admitted under each of the preference categories, the total of which should be within the 170,000 annual ceiling. However, in the implementation of the Act, a "fall down" is allowed in the issuance of immigrant visas. This means that unused slots under one preference can be used by the next lower preference category. There are no preference categories for Western Hemisphere immigrants; people simply apply and are admitted within the 120,000 annual quota (USDOL, 1974:6-9, 61; NCMP, 1978).

In general, the Immigration Act of 1965 tended to favor immigrants from certain nations, as well as certain types of immigrants over others. For instance, by nationality the Act tended to favor immigrants from Italy, Mexico and the Philippines where there are more applicants for immigration than there are slots allotted under the national and preference quotas. There were always more Italians and Mexicans applying for immigration from the Western Hemisphere; and Pilipino applicants always exceeded their 20,000 annual quota. The former two nations are favored by the Fifth Preference, while Pilipinos are favored by the Third Preference.

The excess of immigrant applicants with high qualifications over the available slots tended to be very selective of those with the highest qualifications. Thus, of the 38,491 admitted as Professional, Technical and Kindred Workers (PTKW) in 1975, the majority (61.2%) came from Asia and the largest group (18.6%) came from the Philippines (INS, 1976:44; Table 11). In general, the

---

[19] The quotas exclude nonimmigrants such as students, tourists, exchange visitors, etc.

TABLE 11

Percentage of Immigrants Classified as Professional, Technical and Kindred Workers (PTKW) Admitted to the United States from Various Regions and the Philippines for the Periods Ending June 30, 1960, 1965, 1970 and 1975

	1960 Percent of all Categories [a]	By Region [b]	1965 of All Categories	By Region	1970 of all Categories	By Region	1975 of All Categories	By Region
Total (All Regions)	(21,940) 8.3%	(21,940) 100%	(28,780) 8.7%	(28,780) 100%	(46,151) 12.4%	(46,151) 100%	(38,491) 10.0%	(38,491) 100%
Europe	8.5	54.0	11.3	45.0	8.7	23.3	9.8	18.8
Asia	7.8	8.6	10.7	7.3	26.3	52.9	17.8	61.2
(Philippines) [c]	(11.2)	(1.5)	(10.0)	(1.1)	(29.7)	(20.1)	(22.5)	(18.6)
North America [d]	7.1	27.5	7.8	34.2	4.8	13.3	2.9	11.2
South America	12.5	7.4	10.3	11.0	7.5	3.6	6.3	3.7
Africa	15.4	1.8	15.0	1.8	38.0	6.7	22.6	3.9
Oceania & Others [e]	14.4	0.8	14.5	0.8	18.3	1.3	13.5	1.2

Source: Immigration and Naturalization Service (INS). *Annual Reports.* 1961:25; 1966:36; 1971:49; 1976:44.

Notes: [a] Percent immigrants classified as PTKW of all occupational categories. The total number of immigrants for all occupational categories from all regions were: 1960-265, 398; 1965-296, 697; 1970-373, 326; 1975-386, 194. Note: since 1980, the INS stopped reporting immigrants by detailed occupational categories and countries of origin.

[b] Percent immigrants classified as PTKW by region to total (all regions).

[c] Figures for the Philippines are also included in Asia.

[d] North America includes Canada, Cuba, Mexico, Central American and Caribbean countries.

[e] Oceania and "others" were reported separately by the INS, but are presented together in this table.

TABLE 12

Percentage of Immigrants Admitted to the United States from Various Regions and the Philippines for Fiscal Years 1960, 1965, 1970, 1975 and 1980 [a]

Source of Immigrants	1960	1965	1970	1975	1980
Totals	(265,395) 100%	(296,697) 100%	(373,326) 100%	(386,194) 100%	(530,639) 100%
Europe	57.7%	38.6%	31.7%	19.2%	13.6%
Asia [b]	9.0	7.4	24.9	34.2	44.5
Philippines	1.2	1.2	8.4	8.3	8.0
North America [c]	32.1	47.0	34.6	38.0	25.3
South America	5.0	10.5	5.9	6.0	7.5
Africa	1.0	1.3	2.2	1.8	2.6
Oceania and Others [d]	0.5	0.6	0.9	0.9	0.7

Source: U.S. Immigration and Naturalization Service (INS). *Annual Reports*. 1961:31-32; 1966:39-40; 1971:52-53; 1976:51-52; *1980 Statistical Yearbook of the INS 1980*: 18-21.

Notes: [a] For 1960, 1965, 1970 and 1975, the fiscal years ended June 30th. For 1980, September 30th.

[b] Figures for the Philippines are included in Asia.

[c] North America includes Canada, Cuba, Mexico, Central American and Caribbean countries.

[d] Oceania and "others" are reported separately by the INS but are presented together in this table.

qualificational selectivity of potential immigrants from the Eastern Hemisphere tended to make immigrants from this area professionals from more affluent backgrounds (USDOL, 1974:8, 16-17, 33). Kelly (1971:157-169) reported that the 1965 Immigration Act shifted the main sources and number of immigrants from Western Europe to Southern Europe, Asia and Oceania, particularly the underdeveloped areas of these regions, as indicated by Table 12.

A 1976 amendment to the 1965 Immigration Act imposed the preference system and national quotas of 20,000 on Western Hemisphere immigrants. It may be posited that this was partly aimed at immigrants from south of the U.S. border who seemed to overrepresent immigrants from Western Hemisphere nations. This is partly due to the fact that it is easier in terms of money, time and distance for people to go to the U.S. from south of the border, particularly from Mexico, than it is from Europe. The Health Professions Educational Assistance Act of 1976, which declared that there were enough physicians and surgeons trained in the U.S., severely limited but not entirely eliminated the immigration of foreign medical graduates ("FMGs").[20] It is interesting to note that the 1965 U.S. Immigration Law liberalized the immigration of nonwhite Eastern Hemisphere immigrants, and the 1976 amendments placed some restrictions on the immigration of white Western Hemisphere immigrants, thus imposing hemisphere and national quotas on white immigrants where none had existed before. We can only speculate to what extent this amendment has been directed against immigrants from south of the U.S. border, which is counted as from the Western Hemisphere.

The latest (1983) proposed comprehensive amendment to the U.S. Immigration law concentrates mainly on the control of illegal immigration from south of the border and the disposition of illegal immigrants in the U.S. Otherwise, it keeps the over-all and country-by-country numerical quotas, as well as the preference systems. It maintains and strengthens the family orientation of the basic law, in that immigrant spouses, children, parents and unmarried siblings of U.S. citizens can be deducted from the number of immigrants allowable under the other categories. It discourages the "brain drain" type immigrants in that, except for rare exceptions, those educated and trained in the U.S. cannot convert their student or visitors visas to permanent resident after completing their studies. They must first return to their country of origin and, after two years, apply for immigration under the preference system. (U.S. Congress, Senate. 1983).

---

[20]Although the majority of FMGs coming to the U.S. are foreign-born and *bona fide* immigrants, some are American citizens who for various reasons are unable to obtain a medical education in the U.S. Although admission standards vary from country to country, it is much cheaper to get a medical education in foreign countries that admit foreign medical students (*i.e.*, from the U.S.). Some countries, such as the Philippines where the medium of instruction is English, become very attractive to U.S. citizens who want to obtain a medical education, but cannot get it in the U.S. American FMGs are not subject to any immigration laws. However, they are subject to the same requirements and restrictions as are other foreign-born (immigrant) FMGs.

From a 1970 sample of 5,000 immigrants, the USDOL reported that the immigrants were a competitive group in the U.S. labor market over a period of time from their arrival in the U.S. There were, however, some pre and post immigration factors that affected the immigrants' entry into the labor market *vis-a-vis* the native labor force. For instance, those who entered the U.S. with the lowest occupational qualifications tended to improve their status over a period of time (*i.e.,* domestic servants who moved up and out of that occupation to enter into better paying service work). On the other hand, those who had high occupational qualifications in their countries of origin (particularly the professionals) tended to enter lower or parallel occupations in the labor market and work their way upwards or out of their pre-immigration occupations to better paying jobs. There are some exceptions such as those who move from a high occupation in their country of origin to a high occupation in the U.S. (usually academics). Even rarer are those from low occupations in their country of origin moving into a higher occupation in the U.S.

As Table 11 indicates, the total number of immigrants classified as "Professional, Technical and Kindred Workers" increased significantly from 1960 to the 1970s. The percentage coming from Asia and the Philippines increased even more dramatically. By 1969 or four years after the Immigration Act took effect, India and the Philippines had replaced all of the European countries as the leading source of scientists, engineers and physicians in the U.S., with the Philippines as the main source of physicians (Morales, 1974:71). Gupta (1973:167-191) reports that the leading Pilipino professional or occupational groups admitted as immigrants to the U.S. from the Philippines were doctors, surgeons, dentists and those classified as "technologists and related fields". The latter included natural and social scientists, nurses and student nurses, paramedical occupations, technicians, journalists, lawyers, judges, professors, instructors, teachers, religious workers, social workers and other unclassified professional, technical and kindred workers.

Moreover, the greatest demand was in medicine and the health-related professions, such as physicians, nurses, pharmacists, medical technologists and institutional food professionals (food technologists, dieticians and nutritionists). Except for physicians where females almost equal the males, all of these professions are dominated by women in the Philippines. Women are therefore the qualified applicants for immigration whether they are single or married. If married, women carry the primary immigrant status with their husbands and children entering the U.S. as "dependents", particularly if the husband's profession is low on the preferred reference lists (Keely, 1971: 157-159; 172:177-187; Asperilla, 1974; Parel, 1974).

A study of post 1965 Pilipino immigrants on the U.S. east coast showed that pre-immigration support networks were no longer very important, especially for the professionals. Without the help of relatives and friends who had preceeded them, many had prearranged employment and even housing before immigrating to the U.S. Proximity to relatives and friends was still desired, but no longer a hindrance to mobility. Occupational opportunities elsewhere made it necessary for the new immigrants to move away from relatives and friends and establish new networks (Requiza, 1974). If the group typified the new immigrants, and indications are that they did, family or ethnic-based pre-immigration networks are no longer an essential aspect of the immigration process.

It is also most likely that, considering the educational/occupational qualifications of the new immigrants, they would have some pre-immigration arrangements (other than family or ethnic based), or at least would be able to take care of themselves better than upon arrival in the U.S. and not be subjected to the "California whirligig" to which the early immigrants were subjected. However, this does not mean that the immigrant doctors, engineers, nurses, etc., are not subjected to exploitation as their unschooled predecessors were, albeit less overtly.

The Immigration of Women

U.S. immigration policies, laws and actions tended to favor the immigration of women, at least implicitly.[21] First of all, they were pro-family although their implications were that the family was patrilocal. When the laws were restricted to quotas of national origins for nonwhite immigrants, exceptions were made for wives but not husbands of U.S. citizens. At one time unskilled male (white) laborers without wives were restricted from immigrating to the U.S. (NCMP, 1978:28, 30).[22]

Rarely did women constitute less than half of the immigrants during the last few decades; as Table 13 indicates women have generally outnumbered men by large numbers since 1960. Undoubtedly many of these women were wives of U.S. citizens, as indicated by Table 14. Note that the largest group of women who were initially reported as wives of U.S. citizens from Asia came from Korea, Japan and the Philippines, the three Asian countries that have large concentrations of U.S. military personnel. However, an aspect of the pattern of immigration of women, even from these three countries, indicated that while the number of women immigrants remained the same, or even increased, those immigrating as wives of U.S. citizens has been decreasing. This may be an indication that while the number of women immigrating to the U.S. remains the same, they can now immigrate under options other than as wives of U.S. citizens. This is partly shown by the pattern of immigration of Pilipino women.

The 1965 Immigration Act may have affected the age and sex composition

[21] The only known explicit restrictions on the immigration of women to the U.S. were against prostitutes, "women coming to the United States for immoral reasons", and presumably the female of the species who were: "insane", "epileptics", "professional beggars", "feeble minded" and "imbeciles" (Harper, 1975: NCMP, 1978:22-30).

[22] One of the alleged purposes of restricting the immigration of unmarried males was to prevent what was called "birds of passage", men who worked for a while in the U.S., saved or sent their money to their countries of origin and eventually left the U.S. One of the earlier immigration policies was to attract immigrants (preferably Anglo Saxons or whites) needed in the country's expanding indusry and frontier (NCMP, 1978:28).

TABLE 13

Percentage of Immigrants and Women Admitted to the United States from Various Regions and from the Philippines for the Periods Ending June 30, 1960, 1965, 1970 and 1975

Source of Immigrants	1960 Percent Immigrants [a]	Female	1965 Percent Immigrants	Female	1970 Percent Immigrants	Female	1975 Percent Immigrants	Female
Total (All regions)	(265,395) 100%	— 56.1%	(296,697) 100%	— 57.2%	(373,326) 100%	— 52.6%	(386,194) 100%	— 53.2%
Europe	57.7	58.5	38.6	60.4	31.7	52.3	19.2	52.6
Asia [b]	9.0	60.9	7.4	62.5	24.9	54.6	34.2	55.2
Philippines	1.2	67.6	1.2	66.7	8.4	57.4	8.3	65.8
North America [c]	32.1	51.4	47.0	54.4	34.6	52.2	38.0	51.6
South America	5.0	53.0	10.5	53.9	5.9	51.5	6.0	52.1
Africa	1.0	50.2	1.3	48.5	2.2	41.7	1.8	44.4
Oceania and Others [d]	0.5	58.2	0.6	63.1	0.9	60.8	0.9	52.4

Source: Immigration and Naturalization Service. *Annual Reports*. 1961:31-32; 1966:39-40; 1971:52-53; 1976:51-52.

Notes: [a] Percent of immigrants from the region of the total immigrants admitted to the U.S.

[b] Figures from the Philippines are also included in Asia.

[c] North America includes Canada, Cuba, Mexico, Central American and Caribbean countries.

[d] Oceania and "others" were reported separately by the INS, but are presented together in this table.

Note: As of 1980, the INS stopped reporting the number of immigrants by gender and country of origin, except in a few cases.

TABLE 14

Percentage of Immigrants from Various Regions and Selected Asian Countries Admitted to the United States as Wives and Husbands of U.S. Citizens for the Periods Ending June 30, 1960, 1965, 1970 and 1975

Regions and Countries	Percentage of Immigrants [a]							
	1960 Wives	Husbands	1965 Wives	Husbands	1970 Wives	Husbands	1975 Wives	Husbands
Total (All regions and countries)	8.1%	2.3%	6.4%	2.2%	9.7%	4.2%	8.7%	5.7%
Europe	9.0	2.8	8.6	3.0	10.3	3.9	10.3	5.5
Asia [b]	32.9	5.6	40.8	9.7	14.2	2.8	9.9	2.8
Korea	43.1	4.2	59.2	3.2	28.4	1.0	7.5	0.4
Japan	71.1	3.1	74.0	3.8	47.0	3.4	32.2	3.9
Philippines	50.1	10.6	49.0	11.0	13.0	3.0	13.9	1.9
North America [c]	0.7	0.8	0.7	0.7	6.8	5.6	6.6	7.3
South America	9.5	0.4	0.2	0.1	5.2	2.7	11.0	10.0
Africa	11.6	6.2	7.3	4.5	4.4	5.2	5.2	12.2
Oceania and Others [d]	16.7	5.2	23.3	4.5	11.1	13.1	15.1	8.9

Source: Immigration and Naturalization Service (INS). *Annual Report/s.* 1961:27; 1971:40; 1976:36.

Notes: [a] Percentage of immigrants classified as wives and husbands of U.S. citizens of all categories of immigrants.

[b] Figures for Korea, Japan and the Philippines are included in Asia. These countries were singled out since they have large U.S. military installations. However, the INS data does not show if the U.S. citizen spouses are in the military or not.

[c] North America includes Canada, Cuba, Mexico, Central American and Caribbean countries.

[d] Oceania and "others" are reported separately by the INS, but are presented in this table.

As of 1980, the INS reported this category of immigrant as spouses of U.S. citizens, rather than segregated between husbands and wives.

of the new Pilipino immigrants. The prospects of better employment in the U.S., coupled with easier credit for fares, also had an impact. Whereas earlier immigrants barely had passage money for themselves, it is now possible for the new immigrants to take their families with them or have them come to the U.S. after a short period of time. Table 15 indicates that from 1960 to 1975 the category "Housewives, Children and Others with No Reported Occupations" was consistently composed of about half of the Pilipino immigrants admitted to the U.S.

TABLE 15

Percentage of Pilipino Immigrants Admitted to the United States by Selected Occupational Groups for the Periods Ending June 30, 1960, 1965, 1970 and 1975 [a]

Selected Occupational Groups	1960	1965	1970	1975
Total (All occupational groups, male and female)	(2,954) 100%	(3,130) 100%	(31,303) 100%	(3,751) 100%
Housewives, children and persons with no reported occupations	78.5%	75.5%	54.3%	58.9%
Professional, technical and kindred workers	11.2	10.0	29.7	22.5
Clerical and sales workers	2.3	3.1	3.5	4.3
Others [b]	10.4	11.1	15.9	14.4

Source: U.S. Immigration and Naturalization Service (INS). *Annual Report/s.* 1961:25; 1966:36; 1971:49; 1976:44.

Notes: [a] For purposes of brevity, these four five-year periods were chosen to represent before and after effects of the U.S. Immigration and Nationality Act of 1965. Figures for individual years in between did not show much variation. The effects of the Act started to show in 1967-68, peaked in the early 1970s, and started to level off about 1975. As of 1980, the INS stopped reporting the number of immigrants by detailed occupational categories and country of origin.

[b] There are nine other occupational groups with less than 4.3% or as little as less than ten persons. They are : farmers and farm managers; managers; officials and proprietors (later changed to managers, administrators, except farm); sales workers (exclusive of those included in this table); craftsmen, foremen and kindred workers; private household workers; service workers except private household; farm laborers and foremen; and laborers, except farm.

Table 16 indicates that, except for a few younger age groups below twenty, there were more women admitted as immigrants from the Philippines than men. The preponderance of women, especially among the new or post-1965 immigrants, may be due to the operation of the 1965 Immigration Act (which made it possible to join earlier immigrants) and/or a combination of the pre-immigration qualifications of the immigrants as well as the better job opportunities and easier credit for fares. In addition, married or unmarried women can now apply as immigrants under the Third Preference on their

TABLE 16

Percentage of Female Pilipino Immigrants Admitted to the
United States by Selected Age Groups for the Periods Ending
June 30, 1960; 1965; 1970 and 1975 [a]

Selected Age Groups	1960	1965	1970	1975
Total (all age groups; male and female)	(2,945) 100%	(3,130) 100%	(31,203) 100%	(31,751) 100%
Percent female (total)	67.6%	66.7%	57.4%	59.4%
Under 5 years	50.9	51.3	46.9	48.6
5 to 9	46.5	50.3	49.3	50.3
10 to 19	45.5	52.3	49.8	49.7
20 to 29	77.4	76.0	67.7	66.1
30 to 39	73.9	70.2	59.1	59.2
40 to 49	85.0	85.9	51.8	60.3
50 to 59	78.1	63.6	53.4	68.4
60 to 69	80.0	34.5	59.1	62.6
70 and older	63.7	36.4	56.8	53.3

Source: U.S. Immigration and Naturalization Service (INS). *Annual Report/s.* 1961:31-32; 1966:39-40; 1971:52-53; 1976:51-52.

Note: [a] For purposes of brevity, these four five-year periods were chosen to represent before and after effects of the U.S. Immigration and Nationality Act of 1965. Figures for individual years in between did not show much variations. The effects of the Act started to show during 1967-68.

own, and if admitted can bring their families as dependents or "secondary" immigrants.

As of the mid 1970s the Philippines was one of the few countries where the number of women in post-secondary education (enrollments and graduates) equalled or exceeded that of men (UNESCO, 1970:62-65: NBE, 1974: NSDB, 1976). These pre-immigration educational/occupational credentials of Pilipino women may be influencing the immigration of women at least in two ways: first, women can apply as the principal immigrants under the Third Preference, especially if their educational/occupational credentials (*i.e.,* nursing) are high on the preference list; and second, male immigrants with middle to upper SES and college or professional educational/occupational credentials would most likely have wives with similar backgrounds. Thus the 1965 Immigration Act not only precipitates, but is also selective of women either as secondary or principal immigrants.

Other Immigration-Related Data and Illegal Aliens

Others factors relate to the Pilipino population in the U.S., including the conversion of nonimmigrant Pilipinos to permanent residents (immigrants); and the issue of "illegal" aliens (some of whom are Pilipinos) and their deportation or requirement to leave the United States. In addition to the direct admission of aliens as immigrants to the U.S. from their countries of origin, there are also aliens in the U.S. who are of nonimmigrant status (students, tourists, temporary workers, etc.) which is converted to that of permanent resident or immigrant. Permanent residents are known as "green card holders", after the permanent resident identification cards issued to them by the INS. Table 17 indicates that the number of nonimmigrant Pilipinos who were converted to permanent residents constituted less than twenty percent of the Pilipinos who were given "green cards" for the years 1960, 1965, 1970, 1975 and 1980.

There are two types of illegal aliens in the United States: those who enter the U.S. illegally, also referred to as "undocumented aliens" or simply "illegals", and those who enter the U.S. legally under various visas or categories and over-extend or violate the conditions of their visas (*e.g.,* foreign students who work full or part time without proper authorization). Upon violation of the conditions, they technically become illegal aliens, they are also referred to as "visa abusers" to distinguish them from the former group.

All illegals are deported when apprehended. However, the location, identification and apprehension of illegals is almost an insurmountable task, partly because they are undocumented (U.S. Congress, House Committee on the Judiciary 1975; Senate. Committee on the Judiciary 1983; NCMP

TABLE 17

Number of Pilipinos Admitted Directly to the United States as Immigrants
and Nonimmigrants Whose Statuses Were Adjusted to Permanent Residents
for Fiscal Years 1960, 1965, 1970, 1975 and 1980

Immigrant/Alien Status	Fiscal Years [a] 1960	1965	1970	1975	1980
Totals	3,484	3,648	34,619	36,675	49,025
(Percent)	(100%)	(100%)	(100%)	(100%)	(100%)
Pilipinos admitted directly as immigrants to the U.S.	2,954 (84.7)	2,963 (81.2)	30,507 (88.1)	31,751 (86.5)	42,316 (86.3)
Nonimmigrant Pilipinos whose status was adjusted to permanent residents	530 (15.3)	685 (18.8)	4,112 (11.9)	4,924 (13.5)	6,709 (13.7)

Source: U.S. Immigration and Naturalization Service (INS). *Annual Report/s.* 1961:18-20; 1966:28-29; 1971:41-42; 1976:36-38; *1980 Statistical Yearbook of the Immigration and Naturalization Service* 1980:22-25.

Note: [a] For fiscal years 1960, 1965, 1970 and 1975, the FY ended June 30th; for FY 1980, it was September 30th.

1978:119-141). The location and identification of visa abusers is only a little less difficult, since they can just as easily "get lost in the crowd" and can stay in the U.S. almost indefinitely, until they are located or apply for a change of status. When caught, they are usually required to leave the U.S. within a short period of time to avoid lengthy and costly deportation proceedings for all parties concerned. Moreover, once an alien is deported it is virtually impossible to legally get back to the U.S. even as a tourist. Hence, many Pilipino visa abusers "voluntarily" leave the U.S. rather than being deported and complicating their chances of ever returning.

Nonetheless, the number of Pilipinos applying for tourist (or business) visas at U.S. consulates in the Philippines daily number in the hundreds. Since immigrant quotas are almost filled or are several years backlogged, we can only surmise that a good number of these potential "tourists" are in fact the "documented" equivalent of the thousands of illegals that cross the U.S. borders. Once they enter the U.S. legally they will lose themselves in the crowd and eventually become visa abusers or illegal aliens. Indeed, one of the most difficult tasks of U.S. consular officials in the Philippines is trying to distinguish which, among the hundreds of daily tourist visa applicants, are bona fide tourists. Of course, errors cannot be avoided. Due to the sheer volume of work, consular officials have little time or resources to do much investigative work, especially since visas are generally either granted or denied on the day of applicant's interview. Decisions are based on required documented evidence (which can be fake or temporarily fended) such as roundtrip fares, impressive bank accounts and cash for travel, personal and real property, high paying jobs, etc.; past experience; intuition; and current political situation in the Philippines and the U.S. (including the on-and-off immigration and illegal alien scare) and between the two countries (Spaeth, March 13, 1984).

Aliens deported from the United States are illegals, visa abusers who do not voluntarily leave the country when required to do so by the INS and permanent residents who violate their immigration status or are convicted of crimes for which a penalty might be deportation. Table 18 shows a summary of the number of Pilipinos that have been required to leave the United States for various reasons for the years 1960, 1965, 1970, 1975 and 1980. More detailed data from the source of the table indicates that a majority of these were for violations of nonimmigrant visas (INS, 1961:55-56; 1966:72-73; 1971:87-88; 1976:92-93; 1980:87; 1983). In other words, the majority of Pilipinos deported from the United States were visa abusers, rather than bona fide immigrants or naturalized citizens who were stripped of their U.S. citizenships.[23]

---

[23] It has been known and circulated among Pilipinos, although unsubstantiated, that one way by which most Pilipino visa abusers are known by the INS is that they are reported to the latter by fellow Pilipinos. Nonimmigrant Pilipinos who are able to secure good employment, particularly if this is in violation of their visas, are warned by relatives and friends not to brag or mention their employment and visa status to other Pilipinos they are "not sure of", (and who may not have as good a job), less the former be reported to the INS by the latter out of envy or for the cash award that the INS gives to informants of illegals and visa abusers.

TABLE 18

Number of Pilipinos Required to Leave and Deported from the United States
for Fiscal Years 1960, 1965, 1970, 1975 and 1980

Pilipinos Required to Leave or Deported	Fiscal Years [a] 1960	1965	1970	1975	1980
Totals [b]	535	1,512	2,067	908	1,224
Pilipinos required to leave	486	1,457	1,968	800	1,172
Pilipinos deported	67	55	97	108	52

Source: U.S. Immigration and Naturalization Service. *Annual Report/s.* 1961:55-56; 1966:72-73; 1971:87-88; 1976:92-93; *1980 Statistical Yearbook of the Immigration and Naturalization Service* 1980:87, 93.

Notes: [a] For fiscal years 1960, 1965, 1970 and 1975 the FY ended in June 30th; for FY 1980, it was September 30th.

[b] These Pilipinos were required to leave or were deported from the U.S. mainly for violations of nonimmigrant visas and illegal entry to the U.S.

RECRUITMENT AND INITIAL EMPLOYMENT

Just as the early Pilipino immigrants were recruited for farm labor, the 1965 Immigration Act also precipitated the recruitment of technicians and professionals, although these efforts were concentrated on doctors, nurses and health-related occupations.[24] It is not possible to discern how many applied or how many were recruited. The fact is that shortly after the promulgation of the Act employment agencies in collaboration with travel agencies started recruiting activities. Most of the travel agencies were well established, while an additional number were fly-by-night operators who claimed they had connections with the U.S. Embassy or INS officials and could secure green cards as easily as they could secure tourist visas.

A number of Pilipinos were victimized. Some paid advances on "employment and travel fees" only to discover that the "travel agents" vanished with their money, or that the U.S. government or Embassy did not live up to their "promises". Others received passports and nonimmigrant visas with the

---

[24] Not all the recruiting was for the U.S. Professional and technically trained Pilipinos have and are being recruited to developed and underdeveloped countries, although not all are immigrants. The majority are hired for foreign employment, usually on three year contracts subject to renewal under certain conditions. It is these Pilipinos that the Philippine government is primarily concerned with, rather than the emigrants. Moreover, when they accept foreign employment under the auspices of the government, the latter also make sure that a portion of their foreign earnings are remitted back to the Philippines through government controlled or authorized banks (Gupta, 1973:167-191; *Pinoy,* February 20, 1978:14).

impression that they could work or that their visas would be converted upon reaching the U.S. Upon arrival, they discovered that they could not convert them to permanent resident or temporary working permits. These Pilipinos either returned or became visa abusers, and other illegals had to surreptitiously secure low-paying, unskilled jobs (*e.g.,* lawyers working as janitors, nurses as waitresses or aides, etc.).

Both the Philippine and U.S. governments became concerned with the situation, the former with the fraudulent recruitment in the Philippines and exploitation abroad; while the latter was concerned with the large numbers of would-be workers arriving in the U.S. on nonimmigrant visas - potential visa abusers. Consequently, the Philippine government started supervising the recruitment of Pilipinos for foreign employment. Individuals could still apply directly, *i.e.,* without the auspices of the government, but, they could not expect the protection of the Philippine government if and when they found themselves shortchanged once abroad. In general, those who took advantage of the government sanctions and protection were temporary workers rather than emigrants.[25]

One of the effects of these measures was the direct recruitment by potential employers, rather than by employment or travel agencies. By the 1970s most of the recruiting for doctors and nurses was done directly by hospitals, nursing homes and health organizations with the sanctions of both governments. In collaboration with legitimate travel or airline agents, these U.S. organizations would periodically send recruiters to the Philippines to interview and sometimes give examinations to applicants. Recruiters are now required to specify exactly the terms of employment, compensation (actual amounts and deductions) and the expected cost of living in the areas where the recruits will be working.

At a glance, the salary for nurses is very attractive and quite high in comparison with what nurses received in the Philippines. These salaries, however, are for nurses licensed in the state in which they are employed. While waiting to take and pass the board examinations the nurses have to work at lower level jobs. By the time installments for plane fare, board and lodging, fees, taxes, social security, health insurance, etc. are deducted, the recruits have little left for necessities and amenities. The situation is worse for those who are not immigrants and are in the U.S. on temporary working permits. They have a limited period, approximately three years, subject to renewal or nonrenewal to pay for their fare to the U.S., their return fare and to save money to take back - which is the reason they came in the first place. It is not, therefore, unusual for new nurses in the U.S. to work full time in one job and moonlight at two or even three other jobs. To some extent, the same may

---

[25] Another way by which the Philippine government controls the travel of Pilipinos seeking employment overseas is in the issuance of passports. The government can deny Pilipinos passports for various reasons. For Pilipinos who wish to travel for purposes of seeking temporary employment abroad, a certification or endorsement by the Ministry of Labor to the effect that the person or persons are in fact going to be employed under favorable conditions both to the persons and the country, and under the laws of the country of destination and the Philippines, before a passport is issued by the Ministry of Foreign Affairs.

be said for immigrants who are not nurses. For example, since the liberalization of abortion laws in the U.S., a number of Pilipino doctors employed as residents and interns have been working part time in abortion clinics.

Another effect of government intervention is that once a contract of employment is agreed upon, the employers assume the responsibility of getting the necessary permits and visas from the USDOL and INS. At least the recruits are now assured that once in the U.S., they can legally work as immigrants, exchange visitors or temporary workers. In the U.S., the foreign nursing graduates (or "FNGs") headed by Pilipino nurses have organized to put pressure on the INS, USDOL, other federal agencies, state boards and governments to alleviate the exploitation of and discrimination against FNGs, just as the FMGs (foreign medical graduates) have been doing.

It is interesting to note that while some sectors in the Philippines, including some government officials, are concerned with the brain drain from the country, others are more interested in the foreign earnings of Pilipinos (immigrants and contract temporary workers) and their contribution to the country's balance of payments and foreign reserves - not to mention the fact that this relieves the country of the pressure of providing adequate jobs to this army of potential protestors and dissidents. In 1978, the Philippine Minister of Labor contended that technical manpower was the country's "major export". At that time, there were about a milion and a half Pilipinos working overseas, remitting around $100 million a year. (*Pinoy,* 1978:14).

Employment and Occupation

The latest information relevant to employment of Pilipinos in the U.S. is from the 1980 U.S. Census of Population. Like those from the 1970 Census, there is no way of determining how many Pilipinos were pre or post-1965 immigrants, although the Census also reported the 34.4 percent of the Pilipinos in the U.S. in 1980 immigrated between 1975 and 1980 (U.S. Bureau of the Census October 17, 1984). The employment of Pilipinos in the 1980s follows the same pattern as those reported in the 1970 Census, as well as other related studies done during the same period (Monuz, 1971:121-123; Cortes, 1974; Kasperbauer, 1974; *Samaralan,* 1974; Morales, 1974). Next to the Japanese, Pilipinos had the lowest unemployment rates in 1980, and close to 80 percent were employed in the private sector. Also, 33.3 percent and 25.1 percent were employed in technical/services and managerial/professional occupations respectively, while the rest were scattered throughout the different occupational groups (*See,* Tables 7, 8 and 9). Pilipino women did not differ from the rest of the U.S. women in the labor force. That is, they were heavily concentrated in traditional "female occupations".

In general, the new Pilipino immigrants are competitive in the labor market, especially for lowerlevel jobs for which they are overqualified. In most instances, they have the advantage over other minorities or whites with lesser education. For instance, a person professionally trained and with experience as an accountant in the Philippines has a better chance of being hired for a clerical job than does a native high school graduate, as does an engineer for a lower position, a dentist as a dental assistant or orderly and so forth. Those recruited in the Philippines with pre-immigration employment contracts, albeit perhaps exploitative, are at least spared from looking for jobs upon their arrival in the U.S. Needless to say, a number realize upon arrival that they could have gotten a better job than in the terms of their contracts.

A 1973 U.S. Supreme Court decision which prevented state governments from discriminating against aliens in employment also helped open more job opportunities.[26] However, in 1976 the Supreme Court also ruled that the U.S. Civil Service Commission did not have the authority to promulgate rules barring the employment of aliens in the federal government; and that only the President or the Congress had the authority to do so. On September 1976, President Gerald Ford did just that (Carliner, 1976:128; *Federal Register,* 37, 301, September 3, 1976:37 301; NCMP, 1978:73-78), closing this source of employment to Pilipino immigrants unless or until they became U.S. citizens.

Other barriers to better or professional employment of aliens are language, licensing regulations, citizenship requirements and the so-called "American experience". Since English is generally the medium of instruction in the Philippines, language is not (or should not) be a problem for Pilipino immigrants. Nevertheless, many states and employers require passing an English proficiency test before employing or granting licenses to aliens, which, of course, Pilipinos easily pass.

All states require licenses to practice certain occupations, from physicians to plumbers and cosmetologists. These licensing requirements are not uniform throughout the U.S. In addition, some states require citizenship (or intent) before allowing the practice of a profession or granting of a license. However, while these licensing requirements may constitute a difficult problem many states may rescind, waive or ignore all or some of the requirements.[27] Also, with the exception of the legal profession, where Philippine-trained lawyers must return to law school in the U.S. to be admitted to the bar, board examinations for licensing can be taken with some study or review.[28] For example, in October of 1980, the Sacramento Superior Court ruled that Pilipinos who have become certified public accountants (CPAs) in the Philippines since 1957 are eligible for waivers of exams to be CPAs in the State of California, giving them parity with those who were CPAs in Canada, Australia, New Zealand and Great Britain.[29]

[26] *See, Sugerman v. Dougall,* 413US 634 (1973). Ironically, the Court also said that under certain circumstances private employers could discriminate against aliens in favor of citizens (NCMP 1978:77).

[27] It has also been contended that there are a number of laws still in existence and unchallenged that discriminate against aliens which would be invalidated today (Carlinger, 1977:126, 205-255).

[28] Philippine jurisprudence is based on Roman law, while the U.S.'s is based on Common or Anglo Saxon Law - hence, the difference in the training and practice of law between the two countries.

[29] As this manuscript was being finalized in June 1984, the case was still on appeal with the California 3rd District Court of Appeals (California 3rd District Court of Appeals. County No. 274455, County 22735, March 10, 1983).

What is more perplexing is the "American experience" requirement, especially for aliens who are familiar with the English language, and particularly Pilipinos, who are supposed to be the "most Americanized people in Asia". Obviously, for certain occupations (such as law, teaching, etc.) requiring close and regular interacting with the American public and institutions an American experience is essential. Yet it requires stretching one's imagination to discern the difference between diagnosing pregnancy or removing an appendix in the Philippines and the United States. In civil or structural engineering, one cannot help but express that a steel bridge of certain specifications "is a bridge, is a bridge, is a bridge", regardless of whether it is in the U.S., the Philippines or Afghanistan. Thus, the American experience requirement, although justified in some jobs, is another device to discriminate against or channel aliens from and to certain occupations.

There are a few exceptions of Pilipino immigrants with high occupational status in the Philippines - political, economic or intellectual elites with cross-national or international connections - who enter into similar or even better jobs in the U.S. Except for these few and those with pre-immigration employment arrangements or contracts, the manner by which Pilipinos acquire jobs varies ranging from person-to-person contacts (fellow Pilipinos, friends and relatives) and professional colleagues to direct applications, responding to announcements and by direct offers of employment. By and large, regardless of whether they get into lower, parallel or different occupations in the U.S., the immigrants' income and standard of living (especially in terms of material accumulation) is relatively higher in the U.S., and often these economic gains are in absolute terms. A question which only the immigrants can answer, is whether these material or economic gains are worth the price of social dislocation and adjustment and humiliations both as individual persons and as members of a proud race.

The propensity to discriminate continues to persist, although civil right laws and affirmative action programs prevent their overt manifestation. As long as the Pilipinos are not perceived as threats to the competitive advantage of the majority, they most likely will not encounter gross discrimination. For example, as long as Pilipino doctors (as well as other alien FMGs) are content to fill the medical jobs not wanted by American or white doctors, they will be tolerated and even welcomed. When these FMGs start to aspire to practice in better areas or hospitals, they encounter subtle and sometimes not so subtle discrimination. There is hardly any issue of a U.S.-based Philippine publication which does not have an item or items, in news reports or editorial comments, on the discrimination and exploitation encountered by the new Pilipino immigrants, be they doctors or teachers.

There are also the allegations that aliens are taking away "millions" of jobs from Americans. Whether by design or not, these allegations often pit the Pilipinos and other immigrants against non-immigrant minorities, such as blacks, Hispanics, Native Americans and even unemployed whites. The extent to which legal alien immigrants constitute a threat to the U.S. labor market remains doubtful, and has in fact been challenged by empirical evidence. Immigrants, especially those with language problems or with low or no educational qualifications occupy jobs which most American workers (especially whites) avoid. This is also true in the immigrant with "brain drain" qualifications - FMGs fill jobs that American doctors avoid. Moreover, employers and the country in general get the services of highly competent and motivated workers at bargain prices. The U.S. Congress, USDOL and the NCMP report that it is the illegal and visa abusers who may constitute a threat to jobs that could be occupied by legal immigrants and American workers (USDOL, 1974; Congress. House Committee on the Judiciary 1975; NCMP 1978).

Moreover, studies have shown that aliens (illegals and immigrants) pay more in taxes than they receive in services. Federal as well as state and local taxes and social security taxes are collected, but illegals are reluctant to approach any government agency for assistance, lest they bring attention to their immigration status (*World of Work Report,* 1958:83-84). Amidst the threat of the bankruptcy of the social security system in the future, a pension/retirement expert reported that the immigrants, because they are relatively young and have higher fertility than the native population, may be a new or additional source of revenue for the threatened national retirement fund (*State Journal,* March 13, 1980:A-1).

SUMMARY AND IMPLICATIONS

The patterns of Pilipino immigration to the United States and interaction with Americans and American institutions may be summarized as follows. As a nonwhite minority group, the earlier Pilipino immigrants were subjected to discrimination and exploitation like other immigrant or minority groups. However, the Pilipinos were different from the other minorities in a legal and sociological sense. First, they were not aliens but "nationals" of the U.S. and were in fact, issued U.S. passports when traveling outside the Philippines. Second, most did not intend to stay in the U.S. indefinitely, but merely to earn enough to return to the Philippines to start new lives. Therefore, unlike other immigrants they did not bring their spouses and families with them, and were more concerned with the immediate fulfillment of their needs and goals, rather than with the future in an adopted country. From 1935 to 1964, the immigration of Pilipinos to the U.S. was limited on racially based quotas.

The passage of the U.S. Immigration and Nationality Act of 1965 changed the pattern of Pilipino immigration to the U.S. Not only was the number of Pilipino immigrants increased significantly, but they were now better educated and came from higher SES backgrounds. They became the Philippines' "brain drain". These personal attributes, combined with a changed atmosphere in the U.S. towards cultural pluralism, gave them wider opportunities for participating in the American system, although they were and are still subjected to some discrimination. Unlike their predecessors, the new immigrants were more likely to stay away from the Philippines indefinitely and immigrate to the U.S. or elsewhere.

There have been similarities and differences in the patterns of Pilipino immigration to the United States for more than half a century. Emigration from the Philippines across time has been precipitated by macro economic, political and social structures over which the immigrants had little or no control. The propensity to emigrate may be more acute with the new immigrants, since their higher educational qualifications and cosmopolitan backgrounds have provided them with higher aspirations and expectations, which they perceived could not be achieved by staying in the Philippines. In other words, conditions in the Philippines, more than their perceptions of the United States, was the major factor for emigrating.

Across the Pacific, whether by design or not, U.S. policies, laws and practices welcomed and then restricted certain types of immigrants at various periods in history. It welcomed and even induced agricultural workers when they were badly needed, but discriminated against them when they were no longer useful, or were perceived as threats to the competitive advantage of the white majority. In fact, the U.S. went to the extent of having those already in the United States voluntarily or involuntarily leave the country, as exemplified by the Welch Bill and the proposed exclusion movement and acts of the late 1920s and early 1930s. (Bogardus, 1926:67-71; Catapusan, 1936:72-77; 1940; Lasker, 1969:33-38).

The Sputnik era accelerated the transition of the United States from an industrial to a technological society. Racially based barriers to immigration were liberalized. At the time when the U.S. was needing technical manpower, the 1965 Immigration Act welcomed and encouraged the immigration of skilled immigrants at the expense of the "tired", "poor", "huddled masses", and the "wretched refuse of...teeming shores". When these new immigrants were no longer needed or were perceived as threats to the competitive advantage of Americans, discrimination and restrictions again appeared, as exemplified by the Health Professions Educational Assistance Act of 1976, and in the application of the 1965 Immigration Act (as amended in 1976) by the INS.

The differences between the two "waves" of Pilipino immigration are in the pre-immigration qualifications of the immigrants and the political and social conditions and atmosphere in the U.S. during the periods of Pilipino immigration. The early immigrants were mostly from lower SES and rural backgrounds and unschooled; while the new immigrants come from middle to upper SES backgrounds and are better educated. It must be reiterated, however, that differences in the types of immigrants from the Philippines results from changes in U.S. immigration policies, laws and practices, rather than changes in conditions in the Philippines that precipitated the migration. In other words, if Pilipinos with middle to upper SES backgrounds and higher educational/occupational credentials feel compelled to migrate, how much more for those who have less - only this time, U.S. immigration laws discriminate against the latter.

Also because of their backgrounds, the new immigrants are better prepared and have more resources to make their immigration experience less painful than those of their predecessors. Their educational and metropolitan experience, coupled with better worldwide communication systems, has provided them with a more realistic pre-immigration perception of the U.S. and what they would most likely encounter. For example, through the media, most Pilipinos became aware of the civil rights movement of the 1960s and of discrimination against nonwhites. They condemned it and empathized with the minorities in general and Pilipinos who suffered from it, but hoped (naively perhaps) that they and their families would not experience it.

Finally, the new immigrants came to the United States at a time when racism was less virulent, more covert and subtle and, for the most part no longer tolerated by the body-politic. Throughout U.S. history there have always been individuals from racial, ethnic or religious minorities with high educational or occupational credentials who were not spared from discrimination. It may, therefore, be posited that the pre-immigration credentials of the new immigrants by themselves were not sufficient, but rather combined with some attitudinal and structural changes in race relations in the U.S. which made their immigration less torturous than the "California whirligig" of the early immigrants.

This chapter examined the macro structures that precipitated the immigration of Pilipinos to the United States for more than half a century and how these structures influenced the immigration and initial integration process itself. The next chapter will examine if the same structures have and are affecting the settling-in and interaction of Pilipinos with the American people and institutions over the long run.

5. *From Majority to Minority*

Like most immigrants, the process of leaving the Philippines and moving to the United States and a new life involved tremendous changes in almost every aspect of their lives. For one thing, this meant moving away from one's social, cultural and emotional roots, with perhaps some hope of maintaining them and/or acquiring new ones. Within the context of majority-minority relations, it meant a change from being among the majority or dominant group to being part of a minority group. Undoubtedly, these changes had an impact on the immigrants' identities as individuals and as members of families.

MACRO DETERMINANTS OF MAJORITY/MINORITY RELATIONS

As contended by this study, the contact of immigrants with the host people and institutions is more than just interaction at the macro level. It is also the contact of two (or more) political, social, economic and cultural structures, some of which may have precipitated the migration in the first place. The relationships between the country of origin and the host country, be they political, military, economic or social, do affect the interaction of people. For instance, the immigrant-colonizers imposed their institutions on the host (or colonized) peoples and dictated the terms of the interaction, *i.e.,* as subordinates. When the colonized (or former colonials) traveled to the colonizer's country ("mother country"), whether as immigrants or not, they did so on the latter's terms - as do involuntary immigrants such as slaves and refugees. Of course, with rare exceptions such as outstanding artists or scientists, all immigrants generally integrate with the host people on the latter's terms. However, the nature of the relationships between the country of origin and the host country adds a new dimension to the relationships between the two, as well as for other parties. Moreover these macro relationships can be bilateral, multilateral or within a network of dynamic international relationships. The U.S. has relationships with countries all over the world - former enemies are now "friends" and allies, and former friends and allies are now adversaries (*e.g.*, the U.S.-Chinese relationship since the end of World War II).

The Pilipinos' Colonial Status: A Case of "Double Whammy"

Blauner (1969; 1972:51-110; 1975:338-355) contends that oppressed minority groups in the U.S. may be compared to colonized peoples in the traditional sense. Inner city ghettos and urban and rural enclaves of poverty could be considered "internal colonies" of the U.S. The similarity between minorities and the traditional colonized peoples is that neither have control over their economic resources, political aspirations and destinies nor their cultural integrity. In addition, colonized people and the oppressed minorities are socially and geographically segregated from and treated differently by the dominant group. Furthermore, immigrants from colonized societies usually carry their colonial (subordinated) status to their new country. Pilipino immigrants to the U.S., particularly the early immigrants, fit this pattern. They may be considered as among the internally colonized in the U.S.

The Pilipinos' colonial status in the U.S. could be a case of a "double whammy" colonial situation and experience. First, they could be colonials within the context of Blauner's contention, and second, they come from a country with centuries of colonial experience, particularly so with the U.S. Pilipinos started immigrating to the U.S. in large numbers during the time the Philippines was a colony of the U.S. It was, in fact, these relationships that permitted the legitimate large scale movement of Pilipinos to the U.S. mainland and territories. The maltreatment of Pilipinos in the U.S. was protested by the immigrants, their American supporters and Philippine officials both in the U.S. and the Philippines. Except for a few efforts to correct the situation, these protests were generally ignored by the body politic, considering who was protesting and in whose behalf (Lasker, 1931:273-288; Grunder and Livezey, 1959:248-275). In other words, if Pilipinos did not fare better than Americans in the Philippines, one can hardly expect them to fare any better in America. Hence, the double whammy effect, as a nonwhite group in the U.S. who came from a country that was already subordinated by the U.S.

The effects of the bilateral or international network of relations on individuals may be illustrated by examining the relative status of the major Asian groups in the U.S., namely, the Japanese, Chinese and Pilipinos (it is too early to tell whether the Indochinese will have the same experience as the other three, since they entered the U.S. as political refugees). All were generally accorded the same treatment and experienced discrimination, yet among the three, the Japanese seem to have "made it" in the American system as measured by social and economic indicators. The Pilipinos have fared poorest, in spite of (or because of?) the "special" ties and relations between the Philippines and the United States and the fact they are the most Americanized people in Asia.

One popular explanation of why Japanese have fared well is that they come from a highly industrialized country and possess some characteristics similar to those of the dominant white majority. To wit, the Japanese are endowed with the so-called American or Protestant "work ethic" (Netler, 1946:117-191; Caudil and de Vos, 1971:299-305). Yet anyone with a basic knowledge of history knows that the Japanese have never been and are not now either culturally American or Protestant. Also, the desire, propensity or necessity to work in order to survive or improve one's condition is not exclusively a white, much less an American, cultural trait. Historically, blacks (particularly the slaves), Hispanics and Indians as well as other white and nonwhite immigrant groups have worked harder, under worse conditions and for less pay than the dominant group. It is also a known fact that immigrants (legals and illegals) work harder and for less pay at jobs whites do not want (McWilliams, 1964; USDOL, 1974:45-56; NCMP, 1978:186-189). Although Japan has been and is an industrialized country, the original Japanese immigrants were peasants who were brought to the U.S. for cheap agricultural labor. Besides, how does one explain the relatively low status of blacks and other "native" Americans who were and are in an industrialized country and who do not have to confront immigration related problems such as language?

Assuming that the Japanese are ahead, it might be more interesting to examine the relationships between the United States and Asian countries of origin, Japan, China and the Philippines. Among the three, Japan was and is (except for a few years following World War II) an economic, political and military power in Asia. Prior to American contact with Japan in the 19th century, the Japanese government did not permit emigration. The Americans persuaded the Japanese government to allow some of their nationals to immigrate to the west coast of the U.S. and to Hawaii to alleviate the shortage of agricultural labor. When the Japanese were no longer needed or when they were perceived as problems, the U.S. body politic was very careful in reacting to protests against the treatment of Japanese nationals, nor did it unilaterally slam the door on Japanese immigration. It persuaded the Japanese government to stop their people from emigrating to the U.S. under the so-called gentlemen's agreement.

Japan was never a colonized nation, but was, in fact, a colonial power for over a century (in Korea and Taiwan). China was never a colony in the traditional sense, but near the end of the last century and early into the present century it was dominated by foreign powers (including the U.S. and Japan) who often maintained military establishments to protect their economic and political interests. In addition to the fact that the Philippines was a colony of the U.S., it was the only one of the three nations that was ever colonized, the least industrialized and virtually a nonentity as a political and military power in the region. These macro relationships had their effects on the status of the Japanese, Chinese and Pilipinos in the U.S. (McWilliams, 1964:89-112; 140-169; 229-249; Blauner, 1972:51-110).

This study has noted that the Philippines has become more independent of the U.S. during the last two decades, and that this was partly due to the more nationalistic and Third World (rather than pro-American) outlook of a new generation of Pilipinos. However, it takes more than just attitudes to be independent of such a country as the U.S., especially after generations of social, economic, political and cultural dependence. It is also necessary to have some power, or at least some bargaining position in international power politics. Part of the independent stature of the Philippines is made possible by its association with the Third World nations emerging as an international power block. The Philippines was in a better bargaining position with the U.S. in international politics, at least in that part of the world, because of the emergence of China as a political, economic and military power in Asia and the withdrawal of the U.S. military presence in Southeast Asia (except in the Philippines).

Thus, the more independent the Philippines is of the U.S., and the better its bargaining position at the macro level, the more likely this will result in better status for Pilipinos in the U.S. In other words, protests by the Pilipino nation and its leadership against mistreatment of Pilipinos in the U.S. today are less likely to be ignored than they were during the earlier history of Pilipinos in the U.S. (Lasker, 1931:273-288; Grunder and Livezey, 1951: 248-275).

This was demonstrated by the U.S. government's final action in the case of two Pilipino nurses accused of poisoning patients in a Veterans Administration hospital in Ann Arbor, Michigan. The nurses (Leonara Perez and Filipina Narciso) were tried and convicted by a white jury. The case became a *cause célèbre* among the Pilipino community in the U.S. as well as in the Philippines and both governments took great interest. The case was reviewed and thrown out of court by the same judge, due to the misconduct of the prosecutors. The Justice Department chose not to pursue it further and the case was dismissed *(Bridge,* 1978:58). The disposition of the case was also partly influenced by the changing racial atmosphere in the U.S.

Last but not least, we have to consider the present state and development of communication media and the U.S.'s attempts to be the leader of "free" people and nations and the advocate of human rights. The mistreatment of minority groups in the U.S. and individual incidents of racism are almost immediately flashed throughout the world as they happen because of the freedom of the press in the United States. On the other hand, totalitarian countries antagonistic to the U.S. show their own people only the uglier aspects of American society, such as racism. In effect, U.S. leadership must be more careful and responsive to racial oppression within its borders to maintain an international credibility in its efforts to speak for oppressed people.

All of these macro structures have had an effect on the manner by which Pilipinos interacted with the American people and institutions: the manner in which they were perceived and treated; how they perceived America and Americans and how they reacted to them; and how they perceive themselves as individuals and members of a distinct ethnic/racial group in a heterogeneous society.

PILIPINO ETHNICITY IN AMERICA

A person's commitment to a cultural or social identity may be indicated by the answer to the question, "Who am I?". Gordon (1964:20-30) attempted to illustrate the American minorities' perceptions of their social or ethnic identities in American society with four concentric circles. The innermost circle he calls self, followed by national (ethnic) origin, race and finally, the outermost circle is nationality (American). Kitano (1966:23-31) contends that as far as ethnic minorities are concerned, the less integrated or cohesive a people are within their own racial or ethnic group, the greater the possibility of "integrating" with the larger structure, although he was vague on the term integrating. Erikson (1966:163-170) defines social or ethnic identification of minority groups as a sense of belonging to a group (or groups) with positive and negative historical actualities impinging on these identities.

The Pilipino experience in America does not support Gordon's contention (which refers to white minorities) and is closer to Erickson's definition. The Pilipino is more likely to identify with a group than with self. In terms of social or even individual identity, the Pilipino will most likely feel more comfortable in reacting to the question, "Who are we?" in terms of the family and barangay, than "Who am I?" Moreover, it is not just a matter of whether Pilipinos want to assimilate or not, or whether preimmigration social structures and institutions facilitate or retard integration as Kitano contends, but also, to what extent the host society allows integration and at what cost. At a congressional hearing during the early years of Pilipino immigration, an American scholar and defender of Pilipino immigrant interests, Emory S. Bogardus, contended that if economic participation is allowed and the social atmosphere is receptive, Pilipinos would easily assimilate. The contention was that the "assimilability" and "loyalty" (presumably to America) of Pilipinos was largely dependent on American society.[30] The problem was in the American social structures or certain elements of it that prevented the orderly "Americanization" of Pilipino immigrants. This was a typical liberal order-consensus perspective, albeit in favor of the Pilipinos.

Like other nonwhite immigrant minorities such as the Chinese and the Japanese, the attempts of the Pilipinos to integrate with the majority were rejected and prevented. For their physical as well as psychological and social survival, they had no choice but to keep to themselves (Haner and Reynolds, 1937:630-637). The lack of social interaction with the rest of the population prevented the Pilipinos from adopting some of the cultural ethos and traits of the general population, even in such an elementary cross-cultural vehicle as learning the language. Since the Pilipinos themselves did not have a common language, they initially associated with other Pilipinos of the same ethno-linguistic group. Outside of resorting to the use of exploitative commercial entertainment, they had to depend on themselves for their recreation and leisure. This consisted of celebrating Philippine feasts or holidays, where Pilipino food was the major attraction. Parties and dances were sponsored by Pilipino clubs (Gonzalo, 1929:166-173; Lasker, 1931:131-141; Catapusan, 1940:541-549; 1940:50-52; 61-76; Bulusan, 1946).

---

[30]Testimony given at the United States Hearing on the Philippines, 71st Congress, Second Session, January 31, 1930 (U.S. Congressional Record 1930:2734-2339).

It may be posited that the early immigrants may have been disposed towards assimilating with the mainstream of American society; however, their cohesiveness, ethnic pride and the barriers against their attempts at assimilating combined to preserve their ethnic identity.

Pilipinos do not find conflict between their loyalties as American citizens and preserving their cultural heritage. They resent it when their loyalty to the U.S. is questioned, since, like other disadvantaged minorities, they have demonstrated their loyalty by fighting and dying in American wars since World War I. They are Americans when they are with Americans and Pilipinos when they are with Pilipinos (Monuz, 1972:51-56; 65-70), and feel that they can participate fully in the economic system without endangering their cultural integrity (Cafferty, 1972:191-202).

Following the blacks, American Indians and Hispanics, younger Pilipinos in the 1960s started demanding what they felt was due them as a people, with some visible effects. In areas such as California, where there is a heavy concentration of Pilipinos, educating children to their cultural heritage is no longer a burden on the individual families. There are centers, partly funded by government affirmative action or bilingual programs, where Pilipino children can be taught their cultural heritage. In 1970, for the first time in its history, the U.S. Bureau of the Census reported the Pilipinos as a distinct ethnic population in the U.S. At about the same time, the states of California and Washington also recognized them as a distinct group covered by their affirmative action programs (Monuz, 1972:104-105, 167-170; Morales, 1974:96-130). Pilipinos are included in all affirmative action programs as well as having programs designed specifically to meet their needs in these two states. During his last term of office, Governor Ronald Reagan of California signed into state law assembly Bill No. 3553, which requires that the State of California shall identify Pilipinos as such in all state documents and transactions, and no longer under such categories as "Asians" or "other minorities". The uniqueness of Pilipinos as an ethnic group and their entitlement to being Americans has been established, if not in the consciousness of the majority of Americans, at least structurally or in the political-legal realm on the national level and in states and localities where there are large concentrations of Pilipinos.

The next step to being recognized as a people was awareness that, like other nonwhite minorities, Pilipinos were not getting fair treatment in American society. Additionally, they had problems peculiar to their race and situation. Federal laws and programs protecting and enhancing minority rights and opportunities (*i.e.,* affirmative action) continued to use Asian or Pacific Islander, which of course included Pilipinos as well as other Asiatics. Employment and training programs were targeted to the "economically disadvantaged" which almost by definition do include racial minority groups, but exclude those who, by government definition, are not poor.

Theoretically, the changes and shifts in the definitions of who are poor or discriminated against in American society and who need government protection and assistance may have placed Pilipinos in an awkward position in the area of majority-minority relations in the United States. Pilipinos who fall within the official definition of poor (*i.e.,* below a defined dollar annual income level, getting welfare assistance, etc.) receive the same help and assistance as others within the definition, regardless of race. In terms of affirmative action, Pilipinos can count on their being a member of a racial minority. However, Pilipinos who reside in cities, counties and states where the percentage of Asians (or Pilipinos) is small or negligible may have very few or no slots alloted to them in affirmative action programs when blacks or Hispanics comprise a higher percentage of the population. Being too few to be included among the "targeted" or protected groups or when Pilipinos succeed on their own, they are not subjected to reverse discrimination actions. For example, if an obviously less qualified white male person is promoted ahead of a qualified Pilipino he/she can claim, with justification, discrimination. If a less qualified nonwhite minority person or woman gets ahead, the Pilipino can claim, also with justification, that he/she is a victim of reverse discrimination.

Hopefully, as the second and succeeding generations of Pilipino immigrants spread out into the mainstream of American life, they may no longer have to confront the problem of grappling with their American *vis-a-vis* Pilipino identities. Pilipinos are now discarding the hyphenated "Filipino-American" and are instead asserting themselves as Americans who are Pilipinos. Being a Pilipino in America may no longer connote the bitter experiences of the Pilipinos of earlier-immigration vintage, which Carlos Bulusan poignantly described:

> In spite of everything that happened to me in America, I am proud to be a Pilipino. When I say "Pilipino" the sound cuts deep into my being - it hurts. It will take years to wipe out the sharpness of the word, to erase its notorious connotations in America. And only a great faith in some common goal can give it fullness again. I am proud that I am a Pilipino. I used to be angry, to question myself, but now I am proud.[31]

THE "INVISIBLE MINORITY" AND THE ANTI-PILIPINO PILIPINOS

As noted elsewhere in this study, the early Pilipino immigrants organized into labor oriented or ethnic based organizations to protest working conditions, wages and the treatment accorded them as an ethnic group. These efforts were partially successful, but lacked some follow through. When conditions improved after the Depression and necessity for group action decreased, the Pilipino's efforts became more conservative on the racial issue. However, during the civil rights movement of the 1960s, the younger Pilipinos, many of who were second generation immigrants now teens and young adults, overtly joined the racial confrontation, to the chagrin of some

[31] *The Pilipino Immigrants,* (Prologue) Pilipino Development Associates, San Jose, California, undated. This short publication is an explanatory and question guide to a documentary film of the same title.

older Pilipinos who felt that the Pilipinos had their own problems to contend with, rather than joining or associating with the blacks.

Of course, Pilipino youth, like other non-WASP immigrants, had to confront the individual and social identity crisis. They had a difficult time placing themselves in American society. Were they Pilipinos or Americans? What were the advantages and disadvantages of assuming one identity over the other, or keeping both? If they chose to identify themselves as Americans, how would they be received by other Americans and fellow Pilipinos? Their parents were also concerned that their children were becoming too Americanized, losing some of the pre-immigration cultural traits and behavior they valued most, such as respect for elders and close social relationships and control (Morales, 1974:95-111).

This intergenerational identity impasse came somewhat to a head during the era of the civil rights movement. Young Pilipinos became more confident and were encouraged to assert their rights as Americans, without neglecting their own racial and cultural heritage (*i.e.,* brown is beautiful, too).

Many of the new immigrants had a different perspective on the racial issue, believing they had less rights to make demands than did U.S. citizens. Those with brain drain occupational credentials, such as the FMGs, advocated equal treatment in occupational advancement based on their own professional competence, rather than as members of an ethnic group. In fact, many viewed affirmative action programs, based on racial quotas, with caution and even apprehension. They feared that in areas where the Pilipino population is small, they might be left out of good jobs if they overrepresented the quotas for Pilipinos. Fortunately for most FMGs, there have not been enough nonwhite American medical graduates to fill the demand, and, the few that are available opt for jobs or practices that are difficult for FMGs to obtain. In general, while the new immigrants may be aggressive in their demands for professional advancement, they tend to be more discreet in their racial or ethnic advocacy.

This posture of being discreet or overtly and collectively ambivalent on the racial conflict may be a deliberate or subconscious desire to be an "invisible minority". In general, Pilipinos have not been conspicuously in the American public's mind. Anti-Pilipino feelings occurred only once during the depression of the 1930s, and were mostly confined to the West Coast. The absence of definable Pilipino settlements, such as the Chinatowns or Little Tokyos, also contributed to their low racial visibility except in specific areas where there are heavy concentrations of Pilipinos. Other than their friends, colleagues and neighbors most of the population may not be aware of Pilipinos as an ethnic group. In a sociological sense, they are an invisible minority.

As such, they are less likely to be perceived as threats by the majority and other groups, and less likely to encounter mass prejudice and discrimination. They generally tend to avoid situations where individual discrimination is most likely to exist, or resort to overtly accepting a subjugated status and accepting the claims of superiority by their oppressors as a means of getting around the latter and ultimately getting one's own way. History is replete with examples of what happens when a people at a disadvantage openly challenge their oppressors and assert their ethnic integrity. When the American Indians did so, they were almost annihilated as a people and a culture.

There are areas with large Pilipino concentrations where having a definite identity and being recognized by the body politic as a distinct minority group may be an advantage in terms of benefiting from affirmative action type programs. However, other than the West Coast, Pilipinos throughout the U.S. in small communities or large cities are too few or have not been in their respective communities long enough to have any collective effect on improving their situations.

Being an invisible minority also offers certain advantages other than easier economic participation. For instance, Pilipinos can maintain their cultural integrity or even compromise on certain traits with the majority culture with more freedom and fewer feelings of betrayal of their cultural heritage. An immigrant minority whose existence in an alien environment depends on the tolerance of a host majority society is not in a strong position to insist on maintaining its cultural integrity - especially if this is perceived as a threat to the central values of the host culture. To do so would mean risking a cross cultural confrontation in which the minority group might be the losers. First, the minority group may have to accept the cultural dominance of the majority on the latter's terms and at the expense of those aspects they value most; and second, the minority group may have to withdraw from full economic, social and political participation in the host country.

In general, however, being an invisible minority affords the Pilipinos the opportunity to acculturate by individual choice rather than by group necessity. The less they are known by the rest of the population, the more freedom they have to maintain their cultural integrity and adopt some aspects of the dominant culture that will provide more meaning in their lives. Interracial advocacy of Pilipino culture can be positive through cultural-type pre-sentations. In other words, as an invisible minority Pilipinos can project, instead of defend or justify, their being Pilipinos.

The Pilipino communities in America are not without their share of those (rather a small minority) who refuse to be identified, much less be associated with other Pilipinos as individuals, families or within the community as an ethnic or racial group. Very little is known of the reasons for this behavior, because these individuals rarely associate with other Pilipinos. The causes of such behavior may have precipitated leaving the Philippines originally. Perhaps the geographical, social, political, economic and cultural distance from the Philippines reaffirmed their negative feelings about their country or empha-sized the positive perceptions they had of the United States or of being out of the Philippines. Perhaps a desire for social acceptance and upward mobility in a WASP dominated society may warrant such behavior. Being among the few or only foreigners (but not associated with any of the nonwhite minorities) makes these Pilipinos a novelty and the "darlings" of WASP middle and upper middle class areas and the cocktail circuit in suburbia. Thus, there is a strong and perhaps legitimate reason for not only wanting to be invisible, but to completely forget one's ethnic and national heritage for psychological and other reasons. The motive is to be disassociated with other nonwhite (and lower class) minority groups, but at the same time, maintain some racial and ethnic uniqueness as a vehicle for social acceptance and upward mobility. This is, in fact, a preimmigration, although not entirely unique, Pilipino cultural trait - namely, associating with those in power or upper economic and social classes to make up for one's real or perceived inadequacy or insecurity. For example, we are reminded of the mestizos in the Philippines during the Spanish era who refused to associate or be identified with the "natives" in order to be accepted by the ruling Spaniards.

The efforts to lose one's original racial or ethnic identity could be the result of, or an attempt to resolve, pre- and post-immigration conflicts, some of which may have precipitated the migration. In other words, it may be their way of pursuing what they perceive to be meaningful lives, regardless of who or where they are.

OVERVIEW AND SOME IMPLICATIONS OF THE PILIPINO IMMIGRANT EXPERIENCE

The Pilipinos in America in the 1980s represent three quarters of a century of psychological, social, economic and cross-cultural conflict and change. They represent generations of Pilipinos from varied backgrounds and during various stages of Philippine history who came to America over seventy-five years. Each generation of Pilipino immigrants had to confront problems in common with other generations, as well as those problems unique to their own generation and period of immigration. As a nonwhite minority, they also had problems similar to those of other nonwhite groups. As Pilipinos, immigration and integration problems were generated by the nuances peculiar to their culture; the structural position of the Philippines in an international system of relationships and the unique relationships between the Philippines and the United States; and the reasons and roles for which they were allowed to immigrate to the U.S.

This study chose to segregate the seventy-five years of Pilipino immigration to America into two types: those who came to the U.S. between 1905 and 1965, and the new immigrants who came after 1965. Regardless of which group they belonged to, as nonwhite immigrants and as individuals who freely chose to immigrate to the U.S. they all had to struggle, change and adapt. Thus the experiences of the early and the new immigrants may be summarized into seventy-five years of what it means to be a Pilipino in America.

Interracial Relationships

The Pilipino interracial relationship with the majority population was no different from that of other racial minorities, ranging from covert discrimination to overt hostility replete with mob and individual instances of violence (Lasker, 1931:7; 135; 197; Catapusan, 1940:29; 46; Bulusan, 1946: Buaken, 1948). At one time, Pilipinos were even prevented from intermarriage by antimiscegenation laws. Several factors led to the prejudice and discrimination against Pilipinos, some of which were inherent in the social structure and institutions of the host society, and some of which were generated by the Pilipinos themselves.

Pilipinos felt superior to the blacks who originally came to the U.S. as slaves. They had very little contact with Native Americans and their image of American Indians was similar to that of most of the rest of the U.S. population - or *i.e.,* the "How the West was Won" variety. Pilipinos also brought with them their own prejudice against the Chinese, a discriminated group in the Philippines (Eitzen, 1971:117-138; Tan, 1972; Hunt and Walker, 1974: 93-127). Moreover, the planters on the West Coast attempted to create hostilities between minority groups by using one to break the protests and strikes of the others, even between the Pilipinos and the Mexicans - two groups that seemed to get along, at least socially (Catapusan, 1940:76-87; McWilliams, 1939; 1942; Daniels and Kitano, 1970:78-79).

Aside from the structural barriers that prevented Pilipinos from interacting with other minorities, the former were too engrossed in their own problems to be concerned with the problems of blacks and other minorities. They argued that associating themselves with other discriminated minorities would only bring more hostilities from the majority (Monuz, 1971:69). Daniels and Kitano (1970:30) also contend that some of the nonwhite minorities (particularly the Asians), because of their culture, religion, etc., tended to be conservative in their racial outlook and kept away from racial movements so as not to rock the boat. The Pilipinos' manifestations of superiority over other nonwhite minorities (and equality with the whites) exacerbated the hostilities against them since, unlike other minorities, Pilipinos did not know "their proper places" in American society (Bogardus, 1929:59-69; 469-479; Catapusan, 1940:49-50).

The attitudes of Pilipinos toward other minorities were also reinforced by the U.S. government's official treatment of transient Pilipinos traveling in the U.S. for short periods, such as government officials, students, businesspersons and the few tourists - Pilipinos who had higher educational qualifications and SES backgrounds than the immigrants. These Pilipinos were informed that when confronted with a racial issue while in the U.S., they should consider themselves as "white". Driver's licenses and other forms of identification used while in the U.S., also identified them as white. This was demonstrated by a handbook issued to Pilipino military officers on temporary duty in the U.S., advising them to consider themselves white (Department of National Defense, Republic of the Philippines, 1952). Lastly the Pilipinos' lack of productive interaction with other minority groups was also a result of their own disruptive cultural traits concerning organizational and inter-group behavior.

Over the last decade there has been a change in the disposition of Pilipinos toward other minorities. For instance, blacks were once commonly referred to as *egoy,* a Pilipino equivalent to "nigger".[32]. Today, that term is no longer used among educated Pilipinos or in good company, and has been replaced

---

[32] As far as can be determined, the word may be a version of the phrase, "hey guy", derived from the manner in which blacks were addressed - "hey boy".

by the term *itim* meaning black. At one time, the term *Americano* meant white. Today, distinctions are made between *Americanong puti* (American white) and *Americanong itim* (American black).

What may be significant is that the favorable attitudes toward the other minorities may have their origins in the Philippines. Pilipino college youth in the 1950s began to have favorable attitudes towards American nonwhite minorities. In addition, there seems to be evidence that this change in attitude was and is related to U.S. foreign policy in Asia and the Philippines (Berreman, 1956:105-115; Stoodley, 1957:553-560; Hunt and Lakar, 1973:497-609). It is most likely that some of these 1950 students were part of the new immigrants or brain drain of the 1960s. During the last two decades, Pilipinos have not only joined with other Asians, but also with other nonwhite minority groups in common efforts to improve their situations, and these efforts are beginning to show some effects (Daniels and Kitano, 1970:78-79; Almirol, 1974; Hernandez, 1974; Morales, 1974:95-130).

Another aspect of the immigration experience of Pilipino immigrants occurred between the early and new immigrants. The individual attributes of the early immigrants combined with the structural configuration in the U.S. at that time made them the group that had to undergo the greatest difficulty as immigrants. Yet, they were perceived with some amusement (*i.e.,* equivalent to "hillbillies" by the later generation of better educated immigrants). The early immigrants are often referred to in the Philippines and elsewhere as Pinoys (derived from "U.S. Pilipinos"), and as "old timers" or simply as "OT's" in the U.S.[33]

As the years wore on, the early Pilipino immigrants had established linkages in the U.S. with other groups and among themselves, at the same time diminishing those with the Philippines. They viewed the younger immigrants as upstarts and snobs. They also felt that the new immigrants were harvesting what they had invested in sweat, tears and blood, while the new immigrants perceived the early immigrants as brown "Uncle Toms". The pre- and post-immigration differences between the two generations of immigrants widened the gaps for interaction. Nevertheless, simply because the early immigrants were older, they were still treated with deference and respect by the newer immigrants in face-to-face situations (Pena, 1961:20-21; Pope, 1968:30-31; Monuz, 1971:85-89; Morales, 1974:35-64).

Recently, there have been some changes in the relationships between the earlier immigrants and the new immigrants. Morales begins his book,*Makibaka* (1974) with an account of how a younger and better educated Pilipino immigrant convinces an OT that there is nothing wrong or shameful in getting some government assistance through welfare, a situation avoided by Pilipinos out of ethnic pride and *hiya,* and relates how the younger Pilipino helps the old man go through the bureaucracy to obtain the assistance. Most of the OTs are now retired and their plight is even worse than those of other elderly or retired people in the U.S. Most live only on social security since the

[33] The term Pinoy is still used to refer to Pilipinos who are or have been in the U.S. and also to refer to the early immigrants.

discriminatory barriers that prevented them from getting better employment also prevented them from participating in good pension plans.

The problems of the elderly (and now older) immigrants are being recognized by the younger Pilipinos and the community, and steps are being taken by younger Pilipinos as individuals and/or through formal Pilipino or community organizations which are better equipped to help them. For instance, the organization might determine to what benefits the elderly Pilipinos are entitled and act as intermediaries in securing them (Morales, 1974: 117-123).

Organizational Behavior

One cultural personality and societal trait the Pilipinos brought with them hampered their efforts in the use of formal organizations to improve their conditions. On the surface, this may seem a paradox since Pilipinos have been socialized to confront the world not as individuals but as members of a group. Divisiveness and factionalism in organizations is not a unique Pilipino phenomenon, since organizations are composed of individuals and subgroups locked in power relationships. The same phenomenon can be observed in most organizations in the U.S. For instance, contrary to the common belief of a united front presented by U.S. organized labor, its history is replete with divisiveness based on political, economic, ideological and racial heterogeneity (Spero and Capzoola, 1973:120-126). What makes the Pilipino organizational divisiveness unique is that it is almost always based on leadership personalities, personal, familial, regional/linguistic linkages or highly personalized *gemein-schaft* type networks, rather than ideological or structural differences.

In addition to fulfilling individual and group needs through strong social relationships and networks, Pilipinos have a high regard and desire for status and power. For instance, possession, access to and control of economic resources are only desired as means by which societal networks can be cemented further and to the extent that they are useful in acquiring, maintaining and expanding status and power - as are organizational goals and ideologies. The Pilipino perceives his/her subgroup (barangay), rather than individual efforts in conjunction with others, as the most effective way of achieving group status and power to be shared by the members of the barangay. Consequently, there is a strong and total commitment of individual efforts and resources in the pursuit of the subgroups' interests, thus exacerbating the divisiveness of organizational conflicts (Hollnsteiner, 1963; Coser, 1969:18-221).

But when the interests of the individuals and subgroups are confronted by a larger external threat, the intra-organizational conflicts are temporarily suspended and then resumed when the external conflicts are resolved. This has been demonstrated by the ineffective individual and locally isolated protests against three centuries of Spanish rule, the successful national revolution that ended it, and the return to factional and regional divisiveness when the common oppressor was removed. This was likewise demonstrated by the early Pilipino immigrants, when on a few occasions they set aside their factional differences and unified their efforts in confronting their difficulties in the plantations of Hawaii and California, as well as the naked discrimination they had to confront (Alcantara, 1981; Teodoro Jr., 1982).

It would be an almost impossible task to compile and update a list of Pilipino organizations in the U.S. - as well as in the Philippines. By keeping track of Pilipino publications in the U.S. (and some in the Philippines) for news reports and from personal official and unofficial inquiries, it was possible to get an overview of the number of Pilipino organizations in selected areas of the United States. There are as many Pilipino organizations in the United States as there are reasons to organize them. There are those that continue to exist and are active, those that exist on paper, those that die out; and those newly organized.

As of the mid 1970s, Southern California had seventy Pilipino organizations; the Los Angeles area had approximately eighty; the San Francisco Bay area had at least fifty; the Chicago area had about eighty; and the Detroit area had eight. A number of these organizations represent Pilipinos as a nationality or ethnic group or as ethnic subgroups of larger nonracial organizations, such as lodges, labor unions, civic organizations and professional groups. There is hardly a large city or metropolitan or even rural area with Pilipino residents that does not have at least one organization of and for Pilipinos. Most are locally based and are concerned with local issues or representing the culture in multi-ethnic affairs. There is no organization that has claimed to represent all the Pilipinos in the United States. If there was one, it would not be recognized by many Pilipinos.

It is also possible for Pilipinos to belong to several Pilipino organizations in one area, exclusive of membership in nonracial organizations. One may belong to a professional group, a lodge, a sports or recreation club, a Philippine ethnolinguistic group, and of course a "Pilipino" organization representing all the Pilipinos in the area.

This study does not have evidence to indicate how many of these organizations are splinter groups or duplications. This does not mean, however, that there is harmony among and between them. Some seem to be duplications. For instance, Tagalog is one of the major ethnolinguistic groups comprising close to ten provinces in the Philippines. Yet, instead of having one Tagalog organization, there are as many organizations identified with as many provinces represented in the Pilipino population of an area, all Tagalog.

Many of the intra and interorganizational conflicts are reported in the U.S. published Pilipino news media as news items, in addition to which the contending factions present their versions of the issues, often through paid advertisement in Pilipino publications. Three examples illustrate this major difficulty within and between Pilipino organizations.

In San Salcedo, California, the Pilipinos were the only ones among four minority groups that failed to get some of the ethnic and community manpower development funds (about $185,000). While the Chinese, Koreans and Spanish had their own ethnic organizations to represent them and help administer the program, the Pilipinos had three organizations bitterly fighting each other for control of the Pilipino portion of the program. The officials in charge prudently stayed out of the intraethnic controversy by not releasing any funds (*Philippine Times* December 16-31, 1975:9). In another instance, the election of officers for a Pilipino American organization in Los Angeles precipitated such a bitter conflict that it had to be resolved in the courts. Thirdly, in the San Francisco Bay area, fights between Pilipino youth gangs sometimes resulted in violence and tragedy (*Philippine Times* February 15, 1975:B-5 and B-7; August 16-31, 1974:1 and 19, and November 16-30, 1974:13).

The disunity among Pilipino organizations in the U.S. is widely reported by returning Pilipinos and the press in the Philippines (Villarva, 1965:30). There is little reaction and surprise, since the participants are Pilipinos and intrafactional and interorganizational conflicts are part of the Pilipino way of life, namely the barangay syndrome in operation. The manifestations of this syndrome by the new immigrants are hardly different from those of the early immigrants, who were less educated and presumably less sophisticated in the management of formal modern organizations. Neither are these intraethnic/racial conflicts unique to Pilipinos. However, if a contest were held to determine which among the racial groups in the United States had the most intraracial conflicts and factionalism, the Pilipinos could easily win.

Pilipinos and their organizations in the U.S. are beginning to learn that they are just one small minority group and must unify their efforts with each other and with other minorities if they are to help themselves and contribute to the advancement of all minorities. There has been some news of having a unified or national association of Pilipino nurses in the U.S. Several autonomous organizations of Pilipino doctors in the U.S. were heading toward the formation of a confederation or council at the national level (*Philippine Times* 1974; 1975). Pilipino organizations are also joining efforts with other minority groups, particularly with fellow Asians, as well as blacks and Hispanics. (Daniels and Kitano, 1970:78-79; Almirol, 1974; Hernandez, 1974; Morales, 1974:95-130).

The Immigrants and Citizens: Their Contributions to and Benefits from America

Perhaps one reason why Pilipinos as well as other immigrants, are less aggressive in advocating equality for participation in the "American dream" and more covert in asserting their ethnicity is due to their immigrant status *vis-a-vis* citizens (naturalized and American born). With the exception of employment by the federal government and some private employers, legal immigrants (permanent residents) have the same rights and benefits as do citizens. They are protected by civil rights laws against discrimination (except in the employment mentioned and from voting or running for public office); they are entitled to social or welfare benefits, education (including bilingual education), assistance in securing employment and training, and so on.

However, many Pilipino immigrants perceive that as immigrants they have fewer rights or at least have no grounds to complain about the situation in the U.S.

After all, they voluntarily left the Philippines and no one forced them to immigrate to the U.S. They could have gone to Canada, Spain or Australia.[34] If they do not like it in the U.S., they are free to leave and go elsewhere or return to the Philippines. Most, if not all,were aware that as nonwhites the probability of their encountering prejudice and discrimination was not remote, but they still chose to come. The possibility of confronting prejudice and discrimination was referred to the conflicts that precipitated emigration. As one immigrant FMG put it:

> ...we are guests in this country. Until our hosts legitimately adopt us and make us members of the household (*i.e.,* become citizens) we must do what is expected of us as guests - who do not have the same rights and privileges as the household members.

Generally, it has been accepted that most immigrants eventually become naturalized U.S. citizens. This contention is partially supported by the few studies showing few immigrants as well as U.S. citizens leaving the country to migrate elsewhere. (Axelrod, 1972:32-49; Finifter, 1974: Warren and Peck, 1975). It may be posited that there are as many motives to become naturalized as there are people wishing to be citizens. The motives may be emotional, economic or political. Some people may be motivated by the same factors that led to their migration in the first place, *i.e.,* the Eastern European, Cuban and Indochinese political refugees may decide to be naturalized and benefit fully from their new country, since they cannot see themselves returning to their own countries in the foreseeable future. The motives of the voluntary immigrants may be much stronger, since one can assume that many of them may already have made a commitment to become Americans prior to actual immigration.

Some studies of white immigrants during the 1920s and 1930s showed their major motives for naturalization to be pragmatic, rather than for emotional attachments to their adoptive country. It will be noted that this was before the 1960s era of civil rights, whereby even American citizens (mostly nonwhites) had been denied rights they now have (Gosnell, 1928: 930-939; 1929:487-455; Bernard, 1936:943-953). This era brought a strong pressure to Americanize the foreign born, and naturalization must have been a real (or perceived) necessity if the immigrants were to maximize their participation in the American system (Aronovici, 1920:695-730; Hartman, 1948).

A study of Pilipino medical graduates in a large eastern U.S. city showed that more than half expressed a desire to return to the Philippines. The

---

[34] Pilipinos may also immigrate to Canada and lately to Australia. Pilipinos and Spaniards can have dual citizenship. In addition, a valid Philippine passport, without any visa, allows a Pilipino to engage in work in Spain, whether that Pilipino intends to be an immigrant or not. However, few Pilipinos seek work or immigrate to Spain, except as domestic servants.

proportion of those who intended to stay abroad was higher among those who intended to apply for citizenship and who intended to raise their children in the U.S. Another study of a small sample of brain drain type Pilipinos in a medium sized, midwestern city showed a similar pattern of dispositions towards naturalization. Among the respondents who qualified to become citizens (excluding those who refused to respond to this issue), a little over half were considering applying for naturalization. The rest were about evenly divided among those who did not consider it and those undecided. It may be noted that some of the reasons indicated for not wanting to become U.S. citizens were practical motives rather than emotional attachments to the Philippines. For example, they feared that by losing their Philippine citizenship they may lose any property they own in the Philippines or hope to acquire, since Philippine laws on ownership of properties by noncitizens are rather restrictive.[35]

The INS does not report longitudinal data on how many of the immigrants or nonimmigrants whose statuses have been converted to permanent residents have applied for and been naturalized U.S. citizens. The 1970 U.S. Census of Population did not report how many of the Pilipinos in the U.S. were U.S. citizens; nor is it known if, when published, the 1980 Census will. Nonetheless, the INS annual reports for 1960, 1965, 1970, 1975 and 1980 showed that the number of Pilipinos naturalized have increased progressively. In 1960, 2,085 were naturalized; in 1965, 2,499; in 1970 Pilipinos (5,469) were the largest group of Asians to be naturalized. Among all the aliens in the U.S., Pilipinos were the largest group to be naturalized in 1975 (15,330) and 1980 (17,683) (INS, 1961:80; 1966:99; 1971:111; 1976:118; 1980:56).[36]

Pilipinos have invested themselves in America and their contributions deserve some comment. For example, Californian and Hawaiian oriental agriculture are what they are today because of the skills and hard labor of Chinese, Japanese and Pilipino immigrants. The first major agricultural strike

[35] In 1974, the Philippine Secretary of Justice (roughly equivalent to the U.S. Attorney General) ruled that foreign citizens of Pilipino heritage can own residential properties in the Philippines, provided they reside in them. This was part of the Philippine government's efforts (like Italy, Poland, Greece, etc.) to have foreign citizens of Pilipino heritage retire in the country and spend their retirement dollars in the Philippines, without giving up their foreign citizenship and risk losing any benefits derived from it. However, in 1978 a measure was introduced in the Philippine legislature granting dual citizenship (Philippine and U.S. citizenship, *inter alia*) to Pilipinos who become U.S. citizens. In addition to attracting retirees, the proponents of this measure also hope to attract investments to the country from Pilipinos abroad, since Philippine laws on ownership and business in the country are rather restrictive towards non-citizens.

[36] Each country has its own policies and laws on citizenship based on tradition, historical antecedents and political ideologies. Some of these policies and laws may be based on universal principles, although their application may differ from country to country. In general, the United States follows the prinicple of *jos soli*, namely citizenship by place of birth (*i.e.*, the U.S.), regardless of parental citizenship. The Philippines follows the principle of *jos sanguinis*, that is a person assumes the citizenship of his/her biological parents (*i.e.*, Philippine citizenship) regardless of where that person is born. Theoretically, a person born of Philippine citizens in the U.S. could have dual citizenship (Philippine and U.S.) under Philippine and U.S. laws. There are, of course, ways by which such a person can retain or lose either citizenship, governed by laws or bi-lateral agreements between the two countries.

on the West Coast was led by Pilipinos; it led to the grape harvest boycott in San Joaquin valley and was used later by the United Farm Workers to improve their own conditions. The stilt-like contraption used in the Apollo Spacecraft was invented and developed by a Pilipino scientist in San Jose, California (*The Pilipino Immigrants,* 1975:13). Of course, were it not for the Pilipino doctors and nurses (as well as other alien FMGs and FNGs), medical care shortages in the U.S. would have been worse. Moreover, these Pilipinos in the health profession are providing health care services to those who otherwise might not have been receiving them - the economically disadvantaged and others in large and inner cities as well as in rural hospitals, clinics, nursing homes, etc.

Like other minority groups, Pilipinos also served in the U.S. armed services in World Wars I and II and in the Korean and Vietnam Wars. Most were enlistees or volunteers, serving as individuals and, in all Pilipino units (Wingo, 1942:562-563; Lasker, 1969:61-64). During World War II, Philippine military units became part of the United States military when they were incorporated into the USAFE (U.S. Armed Forces in the Far East) under General Douglas MacArthur. After the war these Pilipinos including those who served in guerrilla units during the Japanese occupation of the Philippines and recognized by the USAFE, were considered U.S. veterans and were entitled to benefits. In fact, the largest Veterans Administration establishment outside the U.S. is in the Philippines. A number chose to stay in the services and later became U.S. citizens when the U.S. Congress passed a law extending immigration privileges to these Pilipinos.

A 1947 Philippine-United States defense agreement allowed an unspecified number of Pilipinos to join the U.S. Navy. This agreement was amended in 1952 and 1954, setting the number of Pilipino enlistments at 1,000 and 2,000 per year respectively. Thus, since 1901, when the first 500 Pilipinos joined the U.S. Navy, up to 1983, the number of Pilipino enlistees averaged 1,500 a year. As of 1983, there were 19,733 Pilipino enlisted men and 379 officers in the U.S. Navy.[37] No information was available as to how many of these were U.S. citizens. However, we can assume that at least the officers were.

Joining the U.S. Navy was one option open for Pilipinos to get better jobs and improve their economic situations. It was also another way to immigrate and eventually become U.S. citizens, in addition to the regular immigration channels and exclusive of the quota system. As might be expected, U.S. Naval recruiting centers in the Philippines (like the U.S. Consulates) have been swamped with thousands of applicants. Earlier recruits came from lower to middle SES backgrounds with at least a high school education. However, by the 1950s, many of the recruits had brain drain characteristics - middle to upper SES, with some college education or degree, although once in the service, partly because they were not U.S. citizens, their pre-enlistment credentials hardly helped them advance (Duff and Arthur, 1967:836-843; Monuz, 1971:107-113).

[37] This writer acknowledges his appreciation to the U.S. Department of Defense and U.S. Navy Department for providing most of the information about the recruitment and numbers of Pilipinos in the U.S. military.

The Pilipinos' stereotyped reputation of being cooks, stewards, waiters and busboys followed them. For a long while, Pilipinos in the U.S. military, particularly in the Navy, were almost exclusively cooks and stewards, some serving U.S. presidents such as Franklin Delano Roosevelt. It has been contended, although unsubstantiated, that over time the Pilipinos felt rather exclusive about the culinary services in the Navy, so much so, that when the Navy started desegregating this part of the service, it was resisted by some Pilipinos, just as blacks resisted integration of the porter service in passenger trains.

Until recently Pilipinos had avoided any form of assistance (government and private) other than from selected fellow ethnics due to pre-immigration cultural traits of self or family esteem and ethnic pride. The Pilipino perceives birthright to assistance and support as limited to the family and one's group. If assistance from other families or groups cannot be avoided, the assistance is sought through third party intermediaries to avoid possible situations of face-to-face shame (hiya) by admitting the need for assistance from outside one's group (a reflection of the group's inability to help their own) and risking the shame of being refused.

This same syndrome can be applied to interracial relations in the U.S., especially as they apply to public assistance. The charity orientation of government or private sources of assistance and the condescending and patronizing manner by which the assistance is extended are simply intolerable to Pilipino individuals, families and ethnic pride. Thus, Pilipinos in dire straits have preferred to resort to petty crimes and extralegal activities to survive rather than seek assistance. Welfare is avoided because of the fear of other Pilipinos in the U.S. and in the Philippines learning of it and interpreting the need for assistance as a shortcoming. Thus, as Monuz contends ... "The American in him will make him want to do things for himself; the Filipino will make him want to help and be helped in the true spirit of *bayanihan,* a concept connoting cooperation or people helping people" (Catapusan, 1939:546-554; Lasker, 1969:100-106; Monuz, 1971:116). However, this attitude against seeking assistance from outside one's family or group has changed over the last decade or so, and those needing assistance now seek or at least expect it. This posture is also a result of the civil rights movement of the 1960s, which shortly after spawned the welfare rights movement.

Familial and Social Relationships

Social or psychological isolation is a problem that most people confront at one time or another in their lives. For immigrants, the problem has a different dimension since they are socially and geographically separated from the people (nuclear and extended families, communities, tribes, etc.) which provide all types of support to individuals and families. For the traditional Pilipino who has been socialized to face the world as a member of a group, this separation becomes more acute. This was especially true for the early immigrants, most of whom did not have their families with them and were barred from normal socialization with the rest of the population. For the new immigrants, many of whom immigrated with their families and no longer face the same barriers to interacting with Americans, the experience must be less traumatic.

In most societies, the rearing of children is the function of the nuclear and extended families and larger primary groups such as the community or tribe. One of the effects of industrialization and urbanization is that raising a family is becoming more a function of the nuclear family and secondary groups, such as the church, school and other institutions (Keniston, 1965:273-310). The rapid advance of society from traditional to modern, or agricultural to industrial or technological has made the generation gap one of society's most serious problems. For Pilipinos as well as other immigrants the social and geographical distance from the extended family and other primary groups compounds the problem.

Pilipino parents in the U.S. are anxious about youth related problems such as juvenile delinquency and brushes with the criminal justice system, alcoholism and drug addiction, premarital sex and teenage pregnancies and "premature" marriages for their children. They are also concerned with the lack of respect for elders and authority, a materialistic outlook in life, too much emphasis on individual rights and not enough social obligations or inappropriate type of independence (*i.e.,* "doing your own thing") without regard for the consequences for others and emphasis on individualism and competition instead of concern for others and cooperation. These are concerns which the Pilipino immigrant parents share with parents in the Philippines, as well as with many parents in the U.S. and elsewhere, but what makes them more of a problem to Pilipino parents in the U.S. is the lack of support from the extended family and their communities in coping with them. For example, when a child or children cannot establish rapport or cannot be controlled by either or both parents, there is always a relative or friend that can help, a source of support that is lost as a result of migration. Consequently, Pilipino parents in the U.S. have to confront many of the child rearing related problems themselves, or reluctantly seek outside help from secondary groups or institutions.

Seeking outside help is an adjustment that Pilipinos in the U.S. must make in their new environment. Another is becoming more liberal in applying the traditional norms of parental control and direction over the lives of their children, perhaps as a device to maintain closer family ties dictated by the constraints of their new environment. In the Philippines, children who openly rebel against the nuclear and extended family risk alienation and even condemnation from a wider network of social relationships. Therefore, families (parents) are more confident that nonconforming members will, at some time, eventually conform. With the exception of periods of high unemployment, U.S. economic conditions and social structure allow and encourage teenagers to work part or even full time. This financial independence, even for personal expense money, further corrodes the control and direction parents have over their children. As immigrants they live in a social structure that favors less control over individuals. An open break from the family may entail some alienation from the nuclear or extended family, but not from the larger society. In other words, the psychological, emotional and social stress of being a family rebel is less acute in the U.S. than it is in the Philippines. Consequently, Pilipino parents in the U.S. may prefer to relinquish some control and direction of their children and count on the latter's reciprocal individual emotional attachments and loyalty to the family, rather than risk losing them completely by insisting on strong family controls and direction.

Paradoxically, one of the factors that may have precipitated emigration by some Pilipino parents was to acquire more freedom from control and direction of their own nuclear and extended families in the Philippines, and from the latter's more traditional values and norms. Therefore, some of the problems of raising children resulting from migration are resolved in favor of what is perceived to be of greater good for the family in the long run. Tradeoffs must be made between the old norms and values and those that are acquired or demanded by the new social structure.

Pilipinos rationalize that these problems are offset by the advantages of having their children in the U.S. Among cited advantages are the better equipped schools, better opportunities for higher education, more chances of getting higher paying employment without a college education, and the improved economic situation of the parents that allows them to provide more for their children.

Another aspect of post immigration life that Pilipinos find uncomfortable is the lack of opportunities to develop long lasting and meaningful social relationships. The high divorce rates and alienation of some Americans, many of them youths who seek other forms of social relationships such as joining communal type groups and quasi-religious groups (or cults), is partly attributed to this loss of meaningful social relationships brought about by a materialistic technological society, which may not be a uniquely American phenomenon (Keniston, 1965; USDOL, 1974:41, 47-52).

There have been some changes in the predeparture perceptions of Pilipinos about Americans after coming to the U.S. This study has shown that Pilipinos interact on a very personal level. Although the interpersonal networks may initially have been precipitated by business or professional reasons, Pilipinos always feel that they are appreciated as persons and thus they expect to be treated as such. They resent being treated and regarded as only business or professional contacts. Not to be treated as a whole person is a threat to one's self-esteem. Therefore, interpersonal networks are regarded as potential lifelong commitments of friendship and reciprocal loyalties. Hence, it takes more than just a few meetings to establish such networks.

Prior to immigration Pilipinos were vaguely aware that some interpersonal networks in America were utilitarian and last only for short durations; *i.e.,* "everbody is friendly, but very few are friends". Most of their interpersonal dealings with Americans in the Philippines somehow exhibited the Pilipino characteristics on interpersonal behavior. They therefore perceived that the so-called American "cold" short-term relationships they heard so much about were the exceptions.

Post immigration exposure to American society has changed Pilipino perceptions. They have come to realize that the interpersonal relations they had with Americans in the Philippines were the exceptions. They now realize that being appreciated professionally or well liked at work does not necessarily mean being appreciated and liked as a person. The Pilipinos have also learned that by their norms of interpersonal relationships, Americans are crude and often insulting, especially when one disagrees with them openly or in public. Rather than take the risk of having one's self-esteem assaulted in an open disagreement, they will avoid such situations. Many have also learned that interpersonal friendships established with Americans in the Philippines are not carried over across the Pacific.

Linkages with the Old Country

Pilipinos in America try to maintain familial, cultural and sentimental linkages with their former society. This is done by correspondence with family members and friends, through Philippine and U.S. based Philippine media, and by return visits to the Philippines. The easier credit for plane fare and the improved economic situation of Pilipinos in the U.S., which helped facilitate the migration, also make return visits more of a reality.

In 1973, the Philippine government and travel and tourist industry launched a *balik-bayan* (roughly translated as homecoming) program, politically and economically motivated, to entice Pilipinos abroad to return to the Philippines permanently or for visits. President Ferdinand E. Marcos' regime called on Pilipinos abroad to support his martial law government. As such, he invited Pilipinos living abroad to come to the Philippines and see for themselves the benefits brought about by martial law, rather than believe the "biased" foreign (especially Western or Amerian) press. Secondly, he asked the brain drain Pilipinos to return and use their skills and talents for their country's development; claiming that conditions have changed and were more conducive to intellectual and productive work - no more interference by inept and self-serving politicians. And thirdly, the tourism campaign was based on sentimentalism. In other words, if the Philippines was out to induce tourists to spend their dollars in the country, why not focus on the Pilipinos abroad who have personal and sentimental reasons to come to the Philippines.

The program consisted of special and liberal discounts for balik-bayans in hotels, restaurants, shops and internal travel, easier customs and immigration procedures upon arrival and departure, and, for awhile, subsidized plane fares from the U.S. to the Philippines and back.[38] Those with high educational or occupational credentials who intended to return and resettle permanently in the Philippines could bring duty-free one "nonluxury" motor vehicle, applicances for personal or family use, and equipment, instruments, books, etc., needed for their profession or jobs in the Philippines. It is not known if the visiting Pilipinos left with a better image of the martial law government, or how many of the brain drain type Pilipinos returned, but the program did earn hundred of millions of dollars for the country's balance of payments and

---

[38] The alleged subsidized plane fare for the *balik bayans* was only on the government owned Philippine Air Lines (PAL). The PAL balik bayan fares were very much cheaper than chartered or excursion fares offered by competing airlines, which resented the unfair competition by PAL.

international currency reserves. Most importantly for Pilipinos in the U.S. and elsewhere, it afforded the opportunity to return to their former country and renew family and cultural ties.

Another means by which the Pilipinos kept in touch with the Philippines was through Pilipino publications in the U.S. Philippine publications started in 1904 with the publication of the *Philippine Review* by the University of California at Berkeley. Over the years there have been continuous efforts at publishing Philippine or Pilipino oriented publications. Among the difficulties (and perhaps the most significant) was the rivalry and duplication of efforts among actual or would-be Pilipino publishers (Bogardus, 1934:581-585; Catapusan, 1940:105-106; 118-110; Bulusan, 1946). Today there are several publications in the U.S. that are Pilipino or Philippine oriented, varying in content and type of publication. Among them are: regular or tabloid sized weekly, biweekly or monthly newspapers; sophisticated magazines, one of which is financed by the Philippine government; scholarly publications on research, surveys, etc., of Pilipinos in the U.S. and abroad; and "underground" type publications critical of the Philippine government.

SUMMARY

The Pilipino immigrants' economic, social, political and cultural identity and status shifted from that of a majority in their country of origin to that of a minority in the United States. One difference between the Pilipinos and other immigrants is the former's society's history of a long colonial experience, part of which was under the U.S. For the Pilipinos, especially the early immigrants, migration simply meant transferring their colonial status to the U.S. In addition to being a dependency of the U.S., the Philippines was an insignificant nation in an international network of power relationships compared with the other country-sources of immigrants. This resulted in the ineffectiveness of protests by Pilipino immigrants, Philippine officials and American supporters concerning mistreatment of Pilipinos in the U.S.

Thus, the pre- and post immigration colonial status of the Philippines and Pilipinos, the lack of clout by the Philippine government in protesting the treatment of Pilipinos in the U.S. and elsewhere, and virulent racism and relative low SES and educational/occupational backgrounds of the early immigrants combined to make Pilipino immigration to the U.S. during the first decades of this century a painful experience. Conversely, the more independent position of the Philippines from the U.S. in international affairs, the anticolonial atmosphere in the Philippines, the U.S. and elsewhere the improved interracial relations in the U.S. and the better SES backgrounds and educational/occupational credentials of the new immigrants made their immigration experience less traumatic than that of their predecessors. In effect, some of the macro structures that precipitated the migration of Pilipinos also influenced the immigration and integration of the immigrants into the American system over time.

These macro structures dictated the strategies that the Pilipinos had to use in order to participate in the system at the micro level. For example, although the early immigrants preferred to confront post immigration problems as individuals rather than as a group, they used organized and group action when the discrimination they encountered was directed at them as a group. Later, as conditions improved, they tended to be more conservative on the racial issue. The new immigrants demand equal opportunities for occupational and economic participation based on their own individual professional competence, rather than as members of a racial or ethnic group. Many immigrants perceive that they have fewer rights to make demands on the U.S. body politic than U.S. born and naturalized citizens. Younger Pilipinos, however, are more overt in their ethnic or racial advocacy.

The Pilipino immigrants' motives for or against U.S. citizenship are dictated by sentimental as well as pragmatic considerations. Nevertheless, familial and emotional linkages with the old culture and traditions, rather than the Philippines as a nation state, are maintained. Like other minorities, Pilipinos have made their contributions to America in peace and in war, although by macro historical standards and impact, they may be relatively insignificant. Whether by design or not, these contributions seem to have been ignored and unappreciated by the U.S. population in general. However, Pilipinos realize that this is part of the price one pays as a minority group member who migrated to the U.S.

Pilipino families in the U.S. are faced with problems of raising children and establishing long lasting and meaningful social relationships. For Pilipinos these problems are compounded by the lack of support traditionally from the extended family and community, and the economic conditions and social structures in the U.S. which foster individual independence from family control and direction.

Although many of the post immigration problems encountered by Pilipinos are caused by macro structures over which they and their hosts have little or no control, many are caused by pre-immigration cultural traits which the Pilipinos brought with them. Among them is the barangay syndrome, or tendency for factionalism which weakens any organized attempt by Pilipinos to improve their conditions. Nevertheless, Pilipinos rightly or wrongly rationalize that post immigration conflicts in their new environment are the inherent problems of migration, and these conflicts are preferrable to those confronted in the Philippines. Migration became their main avenue in their search for a more meaningful life for themselves and their children. Being a Pilipino, American or some form of cultural hybrid is only secondary and is one way to achieve their aspirations as individuals and as a people.

6. *Summary and Implications: Solving Human and Social Conflicts Through Migration*

This study has taken the position that although voluntary immigration is a phenomenon in which the immigrants themselves are the ultimate actors, it occurs within structural networks of relationships and constraints over which the immigrants have little or no control. It can be argued that manipulation of national and international migratory patterns is one way by which the availability and flow of surplus labor is controlled by a capitalist system. Another perspective is that migration is the result of relationships of inequality and dependencies maintained under colonialism or neocolonialism. Moreover, the structural determinants and constraints that affect immigration also shape the psychological, social, political, economic and cultural environment in which the contacts between the immigrants and the hosts occur at the micro level.

The Pilipino experience in the United States is in some ways similar to that of all Americans who have been immigrants at one time or another. Principally, what brought them all to America (with the exception of the blacks) was the search for a meaningful life. Actual or perceived conditions in their land of origin were such that migration was viewed as the only viable alternative to a better life. America continues to offer the most hope for immigrants. In spite of some racially based immigration laws, the United States of America still has one of the most open and liberal immigration policies.

Thus, for thousands of Pilipinos covering several generations the U.S. has been and continues to be the "land of promises". Whether their immigration and subsequent experience has made this a reality or still a promise can be capsulized as the Pilipino American experience, which this study has attempted to address. This chapter summarizes that experience, and from it draws some perspective on the future of majority-minority relations, not only for Pilipinos, but for other Americans similarly situated.

STRUCTURAL CONDITIONS RELATED
TO IMMIGRATION

From an historical perspective, it was determined that the Pilipino immigrants to the U.S. came from a country with a long colonial experience. The Philippines was a colony of Spain for three centuries, and later of the U.S. for more than fifty years. This colonial status has linked the Philippines and Pilipinos to a position of dependency on an international network and to a prolonged state of underdevelopment. The status of dependency and underdevelopment combined with years of wars for independence, the world economic depression of the 1930s, the destruction brought about by World War II, the continued recession after the war, and deteriorating economic and political conditions since the 1970s led to the development of structures and conditions that precipitated the emigration of Pilipinos from the beginning of this century to the present.

In the meantime, towards the end of the 19th century, changes were occurring in the U.S. that would eventually lead to its need for cheap alien labor. Among the major structural changes that were happening in the U.S. were the abolition of slavery, the expansion of industry and family-type farms in the north and midwest, the expansion of the U.S. frontier to the west, and the development of large scale agro-industries. The need for cheap labor was initially met by poor, unskilled and highly mobile males (the "hobo") and some Native Americans. Later, they were supplemented and supplanted by aliens such as Mexicans, Chinese and Japanese.

However, as soon as these people were perceived as threats and competition to the white majority, their immigration was stopped or limited. This resulted in the first U.S. Immigration Law passed in 1882 to halt or limit the immigration of nonwhites in general and the Chinese in particular. The stoppage or limitation of immigration of nonwhite immigrants did not contain the "yellow peril" however; in fact it exacerbated the need for unskilled, low-wage labor which most whites did not want to perform.

The U.S. acquisition of the Philippines from Spain, as a result of the Spanish American War of 1896 helped solve this American labor shortage. A large number of Pilipinos were willing and able to immigrate to the U.S. to fill this vacuum. The alternative to immigrating to the U.S. meant resignation to economic, social and cultural deprivation. The actual flow of immigrants to the U.S. mainland, Hawaii and other U.S. territories was also structurally determined and controlled by unilateral acts of the U.S., as well as bilateral actions between the Philippines and the U.S.

Briefly then, the "voluntary" immigration of Pilipinos to the U.S. was precipitated by structures at the macro level which dictated that emigration was the only perceived or actual means for living meaningful lives. The number of Pilipinos that could immigrate and the manner by which they could enter the U.S. was likewise determined by political, social and economic factors over which the immigrants had little or no control.

The large scale migration of Pilipinos to the U.S., whether the early immigrants or the brain drain type, elicited concern in some sectors of both countries. Some Philippine leaders were concerned with the flight of their young men and, lately, the talented. In the U.S, segments of organized labor, trades and professions were concerned with the threat of competition from this cheap source of labor as were the chronic racists who were apprehensive of the additional intrusion into the Anglo Saxon race. However, as a minority they did not have the power to change the macro structures in both countries that precipitated or allowed the migration of Pilipinos.

In effect, whether by design or collusion, the large scale migration of Pilipinos to the U.S. benefited certain segments of both countries. Philippine leaders were relieved of the pressure to effect radical changes and introduce improvements that would have removed some, if not most, of the conditions that precipitated the emigration of Pilipinos, thereby maintaining the *status quo* to the advantage of some. At the same time, segments of the U.S. economy were provided with a cheap source of labor when and where shortages were felt, or in jobs which Americans did not want.

THE MACRO RAMIFICATIONS IN MAJORITY AND MINORITY RELATIONS

The process of immigration involves more than just the contact and interaction of two peoples; it also involves the contact and interaction of two societal structures. Consequently, the interaction between the immigrants and the host people is to a great extent determined by the structural relationships between the immigrant's country of origin and the host country. The colonizer-immigrant, regardless of numerical superiority or inferiority, always sets the terms by which the colonizer and the colonized interact. The involuntary immigrants such as the slaves and refugees also interact on the dominant or host society's terms. The voluntary immigrants, regardless of the structural relationships between their country of origin and the host society and the conditions on which they were allowed to immigrate consciously or subconsciously also interact on the dominant (host) society's terms. However, the more homogeneous the immigrants' culture with the host culture, the less conflict involved in adjusting.

This study has demonstrated that this was hardly the case of the Pilipino immigrants to the U.S. In the first place, the "free" alternative of not immigrating could be perceived as real deprivation in the Philippines. In the second place, once the Pilipinos "freely opted" to immigrate, they were not as free to fully participate in the American system as they thought they would be. Thus, their necessity to migrate, whether real or perceived, on the host society's terms hardly puts them on equal status with the latter. Thirdly, the Pilipinos were colonized by the U.S. in their own homeland. Migration to the U.S. merely transferred their colonial or subordinate position from their native land to that of the colonizer's. Fourth, until recently, the Philippines played a dependent role in relation to the United States in regional and international affairs, even after its political "independence" in 1946.

It was noted that the Chinese, Japanese and Pilipinos were allowed (in fact induced) to immigrate to the U.S. for similar economic reasons, and were subjected to almost the same prejudice and discrimination. Yet among the three, the Japanese seem to have fared best and the Pilipinos the least, in terms of their SES as of the 1970s. The differential relationships between the United States and Japan, China and the Philippines, and the similar differential SES of their nationals in the U.S., is more than just a coincidence - among the three groups, the Japanese nation had the most political, economic and military leverage to protest the treatment of their nationals in the United States, while the Philippines had the least. Time may tell as to how the Pilipinos in the United States will be affected by the more independent stance of the Philippines vis-a-vis the U.S. in regional and international power politics, the leverage the Philippines will continue to have due to the need for U.S. military bases in that country, and the large immigration of refugees to the U.S. from Asia and elsewhere during the last few years.

The changing networks of international relationships - political, economic and military conflicts of power and alliances - also contribute to the type of majority/minority relationships in the U.S. The development of worldwide communicaton technology also must be considered. The U.S. commitment to freedom of the press, which results in uncensored information coming out of the country, coupled with the selective presentation of American life by some governments to their own people has, to some extent, exerted more pressure on the U.S. body-politic and leadership "to put their own house in order first" before they can condemn inequalities and the suppression of human rights in other countries.

It is also interesting to note that because of this traditional association between the two countries - an association which resulted in an "Americanized" and English-speaking populace in the Philippines - an informal, yet active "favored immigrant" status resulted.

These macro dimensions influence the shape and substance of majority/ minority relations in the U.S., in particular the periods of migration and type of immigrants from the Philippines. They also influence the kind and substance of the latter's interaction with the American people and institutions at the micro level.

PILIPINO IMMIGRANTS AND THEIR EXPERIENCES

The first Pilipinos in the U.S. at the turn of the century were a few hundred students who did not have any difficulty being accepted by the host society. By about 1920, these students were followed by thousands of workers from rural and peasant origins; they went to Hawaii first and later to the U.S. West Coast. However, both the students and workers soon realized that they were being induced to go to the U.S. for the same reasons the Chinese and the Japanese were, namely, cheap agricultural labor. In effect, just as the Pilipino immigrants were not absolutely free in deciding whether to migrate or not, neither were they free to make decisions in the U.S. Like other nonwhite minorities, they were not allowed to participate fully and freely with the host society's social, economic, political and cultural institutions. They were caught in a psychological and sociological dilemma. They were subjected to prejudice and discrimination because they were "different", and as such were threats to the values and institutions of the host society, especially to its racial purity. At the same time, they were denied the opportunity to participate in American institutions which could have led to their partial or full integration into American society.

Unlike the Chinese and Japanese who were aliens and therefore could be excluded from the U.S., Pilipinos could not by subjected to U.S. exclusionary laws since the Philippines was a territory of the U.S. The proponents of Philippine independence in the U.S. gained additional supporters. There were elements in the U.S., particularly organized labor, who wanted the Pilipinos deported or excluded from immigration to the country. They quite rightly argued that the only way to exclude Pilipinos was to make the Philippines an independent country from which, as aliens, Pilipinos could be subjected to the then racist U.S. immigration laws. Thus the early Pilipino immigrants (*i.e.,* between 1905 and 1965) were subjected to the same institutional racism at the micro level of interaction.

The second and current wave of immigrants came as a result of the 1965 Immigration Act, and outnumbers the pre-1935 group. Moreover, they have higher qualifications and have come from higher social and economic backgrounds. In general, partly because of these social, economic and educational/occupational characteristics, the new immigrants are faring better in the American system than their predecessors did. In addition, the new immigrants came to the U.S. at the time when the civil rights movement of the 1960s was beginning to produce some results. For instance, most of the blatant forms of discrimination have been removed from U.S. statutes, and the right of racial and ethnic minorities to be different is being recognized, at least by the government.

The patterns of immigration by the early and new immigrants prevented the development of Pilipino geographical settlements similar to Chinatowns and Little Tokyos. The early immigrants were mostly males who lived on the plantation camps or worked at low service occupations in the cities. Between agricultural seasons, they moved to the cities for low-skilled employment or went to work in the fish canneries in Alaska. Being mostly male and highly mobile, there was little reason for them to establish homes in one place, even if they could have afforded or were allowed to do so. The high educational/ occupational qualifications and higher socioeconomic status of the new immigrants allowed them to bring their families with them, making possible their pursuance of employment and professional opportunities without the help of family or ethnic based preimmigration networks. While Pilipinos do not form particular neighborhood groupings, they are concentrated in a few areas such as California.

Hence, since the turn of the century when Pilipinos started immigrating to the U.S., the Pilipino community in the country is more of a community of consciousness, located in social space, rather than a definite locality-based physical phenomenon. The closest concrete manifestations of a Pilipino community are the formal organizations, which range from social clubs to professional groups, and the U.S. (and Canadian) based Pilipino media.

The conflicts that precipitated Pilipino emigration were perceived as being beyond their ability to solve. Pilipino perceptions of the U.S. were not always realistic; nevertheless, they knew they were not moving into a paradise. They were aware that migrating to a new society would present new forms of conflicts which they would have to confront and resolve. However, their preimmigration perceptions were that the conflicts to be faced in the new land would be easier to confront than those they were leaving behind because they would have more control over means for confronting them.

Among the perceived conflicts especially of the new immigrants, were racism, prejudice and discrimination, in addition to some structural constraints which might prevent them from realizing full professional or intellectual potential (*i.e,* stringent rules for practice of medicine in the U.S., etc.). However, they still perceived that within the U.S. structures, they would have wider ground for moving about, with more and better options than those present in their own country. Given the constraints of both the Philippines and the U.S., Pilipino immigrants believed that the U.S. offered better chances for pursuing what they perceived to be meaningful lives as human beings. This study has shown that another choice for many immigrants was between control by the values, norms and social structure of the Philippines *vis-a-vis* more individual autonomy elsewhere. Social and geographical distance from the cultural, social and structural constraints in the Philippines, combined with their perceptions of U.S. values and structures allowing maximum individual autonomy, made them prefer the latter.

A significant difference between the early and the new Pilipino immigrants was their preimmigration perceptions of the U.S. and the actual situations they had to confront once in America. As noted earlier, the racial problems encountered by the early immigrants were reported in the Philippine media and discussed in political and academic circles, but these rarely filtered down to the countryside from which most of the immigrants came. The officially projected image of the U.S., coupled with the rosy picture presented by labor recruiters, prevailed upon a people who were desperately looking for a way out of generations of economic and social bondage.

Consequently, a major problem of the early immigrants was the disparity between what they were led to believe about the U.S. and the actual situation they confronted. In fact, this discrepancy between the Pilipinos' image of America as painted by Americans in the Philippines and the real situation in the U.S. was one of the major themes of the writers (Pilipinos and Americans) protesting the treatment of Pilipinos in the U.S. (Lasker, 1931; Catapusan, 1940; Buaken, 1948; Bulusan, 1946). This theme is capsulized by Manuel Buaken when he asks:

> Where is the heart of America? I am one of many thousands of young men born under the American flag, raised as loyal, idealistic Americans under your promises of equality for all, enticed by glowing tales of educational opportunities. Once here, we are met by exploiters, shunted

into slums, greeted only by gamblers and prostitutes, taught only the worse in your civilization. America came to us with bright-winged promises of liberty, equality, fraternity. What has become of them?[39]

On the other hand, the new immigrants had more realistic preimmigration perceptions of the racial problems that they would most likely encounter in America. Moreover, they were immigrating to the U.S. at a time when the racial issues in the U.S. and the civil rights movement were getting worldwide attention. Unschooled farmers in the rural areas of the Philippines received current information through the transistor radio, in their own language or dialect of the events in Selma, Alabama and Watts, Los Angeles, and of Martin Luther King, Jr.

This study has demonstrated that Pilipino immigrants still identify strongly with the family. They are not faced with the same dilemmas that some other minority groups must confront, such as the problem of trading off cultural integrity in exchange for economic or political gains (Cafferty, 1972:191-202). Their problem is one of choosing which aspects of the two worlds will allow them to live more meaningful lives. A stubborn insistence on cultural integrity at the expense of deprivation of basic necessities and comforts is ridiculous; at the same time, "selling out" one's cultural integrity for purely material gains is just as bad.

The greater the economic security, the better the chances for individual preferences, among which is the opportunity to maintain a cultural integrity or that of acquiring a different one. Almost all of the Pilipino immigrants to the U.S. across time have had to face racial discrimination and prejudice in one form or another. However, the early immigrants were at a disadvantage due to their low socioeconomic backgrounds and lack of educational and professional credentials and to the fact that they were immigrating to the U.S. at a time when racism was more overt and virulent.

The traditional Pilipino pattern of interpersonal behavior relating to the avoidance of interpersonal friction has served the Pilipino immigrant well in adjusting to a new culture. This helped him balance perceived needs while maintaining some cultural integrity. Cultural integrity can be asserted when needed, but it can also be suspended when necessity demands.

The "loyalty" of the Pilipino immigrant to the Philippines is based primarily on the cultural heritage rather than the nation state. Literature, the arts, music and food that are Pilipino are valued as are those aspects of Philippine culture that give more meaning to life: smooth interpersonal relationships; long-lasting and nonutilitarian interpersonal relationships; the value of reciprocity; and respect and concern for the old. Identity concerns of the Pilipino center on how these values may be maintained while allowing pursuance of economic goals. Pilipinos are proud to be American citizens, especially when they are in the Philippines. However, they are also proud of their Philippine cultural heritage.

There was and is a "community of consciousness" among Pilipinos in the

[39] *New Republic*, September 23, 1940. Quoted in McWilliams, 1964:248.

U.S., but only in the most abstract sense. However, intraethnic conflicts among Pilipinos and the tendency to identify with smaller groups rather than with ethnicity, as well as the preimmigration heterogeneity of the Pilipinos, is still a basic reality.

Regardless of their feelings and attitudes about the Philippines at the time of emigration, social and geographical distance has made them more conscious of being Pilipinos. When conflict was their reason for leaving the Philippines, distance only reaffirmed negative feelings about the Philippines and accentuated positive perceptions of the U.S. As one Pilipino academician who completed his graduate studies in the U.S. and traveled extensively in Europe and Asia put it:

> ... for them nothing is right in the Philippines and everything is okay in the U.S., or for that matter, everything will be all right anywhere else except the Philippines. They are the unhappiest of the lot, in spite of their TV sets, two cars, and aping of upper-middle class WASP lifestyles. They deny their heritage and race, but do not realize that these do not change the facts, at least as far as the Anglos are concerned. They are like the "mestizos" in the Philippines. In their struggle to deny their original heritage, they miss the chance of being first class human beings and Pilipinos. Instead, they end up being second class Americans and third class human beings.

Although not expressed as bitterly and as explicitly as the above, many Pilipinos harbor similar sentiments towards fellow Pilipinos who, for one reason or another, have bad feelings about their former country, at the same time conceding that there could be legitimate reasons for feeling that way.

The Vietnam War, the civil rights and black movement of the 1960s, the rhetoric and publicity on neocolonialism, and the U.S. and "Western" foreign policy have all changed the perceptions of Pilipinos about themselves and their relations with other minority groups in the U.S. and other oppressed peoples in the Third World. Pilipinos on the West Coast are already moving towards acting in common with other Asians. The rhetoric on the issues they have to confront has now shifted from "Pilipino Americans" to "Asian Americans". Observers believe that the direction will be towards identification as disadvantaged Americans (Daniels and Kitano, 1966:29-31 and 1970:78-79 and 102-120; and Morales, 1974:127-130).

There is no doubt that the improved racial atmosphere in the United States since the civil rights movement of the 1960s and the higher qualifications of the new immigrants contributed to the better reception they experienced when they immigrated. In addition, it is a fact that during the same period the Philippines was also becoming more independent of the U.S.

SOME CONCEPTUAL CONSIDERATIONS

Like most studies on human behavior, this one has uncovered more questions than the answers it sought. The questions uncovered and the directions in which possible answers might be found are as many and varied as the interests, preferences and personal biases of those concerned with the issues of migration and majority-minority relations. Nevertheless, it has generated some conceptual constructs, many not new or original, but tending to support previous theories and contentions. They shall be discussed briefly for whatever aid they may give to understanding majority and minority relations and the immigration process.

One such perspective as supported by the findings of this study is that a large portion of majority population in a given society, at a given time, may not be prejudiced against any one or other minority group, be it on racial, religious, political, national origins, age or sexual grounds. Yet these same people, wittingly or unwittingly, do practice some form of discrimination - what Kitano calls (1966:23-31) the "passive discrimination" of the normal person. In other words, people may be aware of a discrimination toward a group or groups. However, as long as the practice does not adversely affect them, the existence of the practice benefits them, or protestations against such discrimination would affect them adversely, they will tend to tolerate and even justify the *status quo* - their "conscience is clear", they are not prejudiced against people, there is nothing they can do about it, and so on. From our perspective it can be argued that since the "average majority" person has no control over the development of the macro structures that created institutionalized inequalities, there may be little that person can do to change it. On the other hand, history has shown that people can affect changes in the social, economic and political structures, if they have the will, albeit at a great individual and social cost. The fact is that the majority (and even some minority groups) do benefit from institutional inequalities, or at least are not adversely and directly affected by their existence.

Another conceptual view is that discrimination is created by, or is a product of, a system or systems, rather than of prejudiced people. For instance, a neo-Marxist view is that racism, prejudice and the resultant discrimination are ways by which a capitalist system exploits people and resources (Cox, 1970; Reich, 1971; Tabb, 1971:431-444). This may be the case in some instances, in some societies and during certain periods of time. However, the truth is that the subjugation and exploitation of peoples and nations by others pre-dated capitalism and Marx.

The data examined by this study that the macro dimensions affecting majority/minority relations, as demonstrated by the Pilipino immigration experience in the U.S. may be capsulized as follows: First, the changing macro structures in the country of origin (the Philippines) and destination (United States) of immigrants precipitated the periods of migration and type of immigrants. Second, the changing structural relationships in the Philippines in particular and the changes in the international network of relationships, power conflicts and alliances in general, also influence the manner by which those affected interact with each other. Thus, as the macro structures change, so do strategies utilized in dealing with each other at the micro level.

Undoubtedly, the United States continues to be attractive as the land of opportunity and, in fact, is to many in terms of realizing their aspirations. In addition, it also has some of the most liberal immigration and naturalization policies, laws and practices and continues to be a major destination for immigrants. However, this study supports other studies which indicate that conditions in the Philippines are a better predictor of Pilipino migration than the perceived conditions in the U.S. This is evident in the Pilipinos' propensity to migrate (either as permanent immigrants or temporary workers) to countries other than the U.S. In other words, it is the "push" rather than the "pull" factors that mostly determine migration.

A concept that was popular among certain segments in America during the 1960s and early 1970s was to compare the internal migration of nonwhites to urban centers in the north and east with the earlier migration of whites from Europe. It was felt that the early immigrants could pull themselves out of their conditions of inequality from the time of their (or their parents') arrival, there is no reason why the "new immigrants" (blacks, Hispanics, Indians and Asians) couldn't. However, the proponents of this view ignored the fact that while the European immigrants were white, the "new" immigrants are not. Secondly, as noted by this study, blacks and other nonwhite immigrants were brought or allowed to immigrate to this country for specific economic motives. As Blauner (1972:2-11) points out, this perspective conveniently assumed that inequalities in the U.S. would eventually be removed through economic reductionism, while ignoring the historical and current social realities of racism.

This somewhat "assimilationist" conceptualization resembles the position taken by whites who opposed slavery and racial inequalities. Despite good intentions and the quasireligious/moral grounds of their advocacy for racial equality, much was based on the perceived supremacy of the white race and culture. Their position was that nonwhites should be given the opportunity to be like and assimilate with the white race, and only then could they participate fully in the American system. No wonder the blacks became "an Americans Dilemma". How does one extend equality, much less assimilate a people who are not and refuse to be white, physically and culturally? So it was with the Pilipinos who tried to maintain their cultural integrity, partly because they were barred from interacting fully with the dominant culture and partly by choice. Nevertheless, regardless of their motives and assumptions, the efforts by this minority of white Americans to eliminate racial inequalities helped prevent the minorities from being totally subjugated at all times.

What is often ignored in scholarly and popular literature as well as in the political rhetoric concerning the struggles of disadvantaged groups is that attempts for equality would have been more difficult, if not impossible, without the support of certain segments of the dominant group. Domination of one group of people by others can only be complete and total if the superordinate status of one group is totally supported by all the members of the group. Americans sometimes forget that their own independence could have been more difficult if they did not have the support of certain sectors of the British body-politic and public.

The domination and exploitation of nonwhite minority groups in the United States never enjoyed the total and complete support of the white majority. Whites from various walks of life have always opposed the exploitation of slavery and discrimination against white and nonwhite minority groups for various reasons. Admittedly, they were in the minority in their own group, and these made their sympathies and support for the disadvantaged groups more difficult and the resulting conflict more costly. Whereas the subjugated groups had to confront a white establishment, their white supporters had to confront their own people and live with the economic, social, political and human consequences of their "betrayal".

The findings of this study tend to support some concepts of the conflict and change model, and the role that conflict plays in human and societal development, among which are: 1) certain forms of conflict lead to or are by themselves forms of association and 2) the resolution of conflicts leads more to changes in structural and social relationships than does consensus (Sorel, 1925; Simmerl, 1955; Coser, 1956: Dahrendorf, 1958:115-127; Marx, 1969:206-207).

For instance, the universal conflict confronted by the inhabitants of the Philippine archipelago during more than three centuries of colonization led to the development of national consciousness. This in turn led to the formation of a nation state, the Philippines, out of heterogeneously linguistic people living in politically autonomous groups.

Also, despite the racial and ethnic diversity of the nonwhite immigrant minorities in America and the efforts of the white established majority to keep them apart, there have been strong indications these racially, ethnically and culturally diverse minorities are now uniting their efforts in confronting the racial/ethnic barriers that prevented their full participation in American society and their development as individuals and/or ethnic groups.

The changes in the body-politic and in the general atmosphere recognizing the rights of the minorities and allowing them wider participation in American society were not brought about by voluntary concession of the white establishment or by consensus; they were the results of conflicts which were played out in the courts, legislatures and on the streets, often accompanied by violence and tragedy. In the case of the nonwhite voluntary immigrants, the conflicts transcend U.S. political and sociological boundaries. Conflicts associated with the rights of minorities did not end with favorable court decisions nor the passage of laws recognizing them. Their implementations are again wrought with conflicts, as evidenced by the school busing and "reverse discrimination" issues.

The historical and current field data examined by this study indicate the inadequacy of the order-consensus model and the structural/functional approach in understanding the perceptions and experiences of immigrants, particularly the nonwhite immigrants in American society. The proponents of this model and approach, wittingly or unwittingly but conveniently, ignore the conflicts that minorities had to confront in their efforts to participate in the American system. Each gain led to more conflicts and, as noted previously, every single right and concession, from educational opportunities to economic participation, had to be fought for at the price of physical survival and cultural integrity. Why then should the white American establishment be surprised if the minorities have not been assimilated into the

American mainstream - unless of course, their interpretation of integration or assimilation is the minorities' acceptance of their "proper places" in a racially and economically stratified society? How conceptually and empirically convenient it would be if the minorities, in consensus with the majority, were willing to assimilate with American society by accepting the unfair and oppressive economic, social, political and cultural dominance of the white majority.

Each society assumes that its society, culture, values, norms and social structures are more desirable than others. Deviations from this assumption are perceived as threats to the existence of that society. The deviations can come from inside the society or externally, as from the influx of large immigrant groups. The tendency to make deviants conform to what the society values most is a legitimate concern which is practiced by most, if not all, societies.

Besides recognizing the right of an individual or group to exercise full potential, a major issue in majority-minority relations that must be defined is the most effective means for inducing divergent peoples to appreciate and conform to the values offered by the dominant host society.

What the host society must assess is which would be more beneficial - exerting pressure on minority groups to conform at any price or allowing the minority groups to conform on their own terms through greater personal, social, economic and cultural freedom.

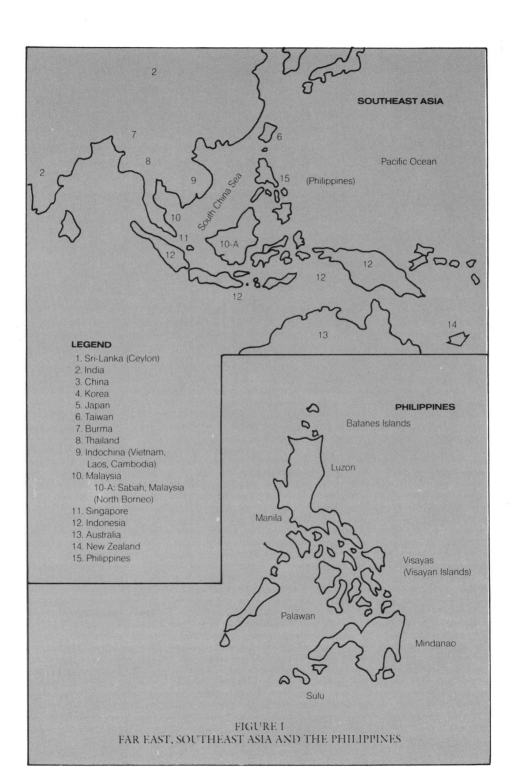

SOUTHEAST ASIA

Pacific Ocean

(Philippines)

South China Sea

LEGEND
1. Sri-Lanka (Ceylon)
2. India
3. China
4. Korea
5. Japan
6. Taiwan
7. Burma
8. Thailand
9. Indochina (Vietnam,
   Laos, Cambodia)
10. Malaysia
    10-A: Sabah, Malaysia
    (North Borneo)
11. Singapore
12. Indonesia
13. Australia
14. New Zealand
15. Philippines

PHILIPPINES

Batanes Islands

Luzon

Manila

Visayas
(Visayan Islands)

Palawan

Mindanao

Sulu

FIGURE I
FAR EAST, SOUTHEAST ASIA AND THE PHILIPPINES

References

Abella, D.
1971 "From 'Indio' to Filipino". Paper presented at the 5th Conference on Asian History, Manila.

Adams, W., ed.
1968 *The Brain Drain.* New York: MacMillan Company.

Achutegui, P.S. de, S.J. and M.A. Bernad, S.J.
1960 *The Religious Coup D'Etat 1898-1901 - A Documentary History.* Quezon City: Ateneo de Manila University Press.

Agoncillo, T.A.
1956 *The Revolt of the Masses.* Quezon City: University of the Philippines Press.

Agoncillo, T.A. and O.M. Alfonso
1967 *History of the Filipino People.* Quezon City: Malaya Books.

Alcantara, R.R.
1981 *Sakada: Filipino Adaptation in Hawaii.* Washington, D.C.: University Press of America.

Allen, J.P.
1977 "Recent Immigration from the Philippines and Filipino Communities in the United States", *Geographical Review,* 67(2):195-208. April.

Almirol, E.B.
1974   "Filipino Aspirations: Balancing Social Pressures and Ethnic Images". Paper presented at the Conference on International Migration from the Philippines, East-West Center, Honolulu, Hawaii. June 10-14.

Anderson, G.M.
1971   Speaking for the consideration and passage of H.R.12208, 92nd Congress, 1st Session. *Congressional Record* 117(36):46602-46604, December 13, Washington, D.C.: U.S. Government Printing Office.

Anderson, J.
1978   "Bureaucratic Delays Ravage Cancer Patients". *The State Journal,* December 6.

Anthony, D.E.
1931-32   "Filipino Labor in Central California", *Sociology and Social Research,* 16:149-156.

Aronovici, C.
1920   "Americanization: Its Meaning and Function", *American Journal of Sociology,* 25(6):695-730. May.

Asperilla, P.F.
1974   "The Mobility of Filipino Nurses". Paper presented at the Conference on International Migration from the Philippines, East-West Center, Honolulu, Hawaii. June 10-14.

Axelrod, B.
1972   "Historical Studies of Emigration from the United States", *International Migration Review,* 6(1):32-49. Spring.

Balitaan
1975   "The Newly Arrived Immigrants (Professionals)". May.

Baran, P. and P. Sweezy
1972   "The Multinational Corporation and Modern Imperialism". In *The Capitalist. System.* Edited by R.C. Edwards, *et al.* Englewood Cliffs, New Jersey: Prentice-Hall, Inc. Pp. 345-442.

Barnet, R.J.
1974   *Global Reach: The Power of Multinational Corporations.* New York: Simon and Schuster.

Bello, W.
1983   "The Philippine Bases are Critical Elements in U.S. Strategies for Local Wars of Intervention and for Global Nuclear Confrontation", *Southeast Asia Chronicle,* Issue No. 89, 3-16. April.

Bello, W., D. Kingley and E. Elinson
1982   *Development Debacle: The World Bank in the Philippines.* San Francisco: Institute for Food and Development Policy.

Bello, W.F. *et al.*
1969   "Brain Drain in the Philippines", *Modernization: Its Impact in the Philippines.* Institute of Philippine Culture (IPC) Papers No. 7. Quezon City: Ateneo de Manila University Press.

Bernard, J.
1971   "The Conceptualization of Intergroup Relations with Special Reference to Conflict". *Racial Conflict: Tension and Change in American Society.* Edited by G.T. Marx. Boston: Little, Brown and Company. Pp. 23-31.

Berreman, J.V.
1956   "Filipino Identification with American Minorities", *Research Studies State College of*

Washington, 105-115. June.

Blair, E.H. and J.A. Robertson
1903   *The Philippine Islands: 1493-1803.* Cleveland: Arthur H. Clark Company.

Blauner, R.
1975   "Colonized and Immigrants Minorities". In *Majority and Minority.* Edited by Norman R. Yetman and C. Hoy Steele. Boston: Allyn and Bacon, Inc. Pp. 338-355.

1972   *Racial Oppression in America.* New York: Harper and Row.

1969   "Internal Colonialism and Ghetto Revolt", *Social Problems.* 16(4). Spring.

Bogardus, E.S.
1936   "Filipino Repatriation", *Sociology and Social Research,* 21:67-71. September-October.

1934   "The Filipino Press in the United States", *Sociology and Social Research,* 18:581-585. July-August.

1929a   "American Attitudes Towards Filipinos", *Sociology and Social Research,* 14(1):472-479. September-October.

1929b   "Filipino Immigrant Attitudes", *Sociology and Social Research,* 14:469-479. September-October.

Bridge
1978   "Narcisp/Perez". 6(1):58.

Buaken, M.
1948   *I Have Lived with the American People.* Caldwell, Idaho: The Caxton Printers, Ltd.

1943   "Our Love for Freedom: 1200 of the First Filipino Infantry Takes Oath of Allegiance Which Makes Them U.S. Citizens". *Asia,* 43(6):357-359. June.

Buduhan, C.
1974   "Two Filipino Immigrant Communities: A Comparative Study of Garment Workers in Winnipeg and Professionals in Vancouver". Paper presented at the Conference on International Migration from the Philippines, East-West Center, Honolulu, Hawaii. June 10-14.

Bulatao, J. C., S.J.
1966   *Split-Level Christianity.* Quezon City: Ateneo de Manila University Press.

1964   "Hiya". *Philippines Studies,* 12(3):424-438. July.

Bulusan, C.
1973   *America Is the Heart.* Seattle: University of Washington Press.

Burma, J.
1951   "The Background of the Current Situation of Filipino-Americans", *Social Forces,* 30(1):42-48. October.

Cafferty, P.,S.J.
1972 "Spanish-Speaking Americans: Economic Assimilation or Cultural Identity". In *Pieces of a Dream*. Edited by M.S. Wenk, *et al.* Staten Island, N.Y.: Center for Migration Studies. Pp. 191-202.

California, State of, 3rd District Court of Appeals
March 10, 1983   County No. 274455, Civil 22735. *Filipino Accountants Association, Inc., et al. v. State Board of Accountancy, and Individual Members thereof.*

Carlinger, D.
1977   *The Rights of Aliens.* New York: Avon Books.

Carrol, J.J., S.J.
1970   *Philippine Institutions.* Manila: Solidaridad Publishing House.

_____
1968   *Changing Patterns of Social Structure in the Philippines: 1896-1963.* Quezon City: Ateneo de Manila University Press.

Catapusan, B.T.
1940a   "Leisure-Time of Filipino Immigrants", *Sociology and Social Research,* 24:541-549. July-August.

_____
1940b   "The Social Adjustment of Filipinos in the United States". Ph. D. dissertation. University of Southern California.

_____
1939   "Filipino Immigrants and Public Relief of the United States", *Sociology and Social Research,* 23:546-554. July-August.

_____
1936   "Filipino Repatriates in the Philippines", *Sociology and Social Research,* 21:72-77. September-October.

Caudill, W. and G. de Vos
1971   "Achievement, Culture and Personality: The Case of Japanese Americans". In *Majority and Minority.* Edited by N.R. Yetman and C.H. Steele. Boston: Allyn and Bacon, Inc. Pp. 299-305.

Central Committee, The April 6th Liberation Movement
(n.d.)   *The Philippine Struggle.* San Francisco: Filipino Information Service.

Corpus, O.D.
1965   *The Philippines.* Englewood Cliffs, N.J.: Prentice-Hall, Inc.

Cortes, J.R.
1969   "Factors Associated with the Migration of High-Level Persons from the Philippines to the U   " Ph.D. dissertation. Stanford University.

Coser, L.A.
1971   "Some Sociological Aspects of Conflict". In *Racial Conflict and Change in American Society.* Edited by G.T. Marx. Boston: Little, Brown and Company. Pp. 14-20.

_____
1956   *The Functions of Social Conflict.* Glencoe, Il: The Free Press.

Cox, O.C.
1970   *Caste, Class and Race.* New York: Monthly Review Press.

Dahrendorf, R.
1958   "Out of Utopia: Toward a Reorientation of Social Analysis", *American Journal of Sociology,*
        64(2):115-127. September.

Daniels, R. and H.H. Kitano
1970   *Racism in America.* Englewood Cliffs, N.J.: Prentice-Hall, Inc.

Diokno, J.W.
1980   "U.S. Policy and Presence in East Asia: An Insider's View". Keynote address at the
        Conference, "U.S. Policy in East Asia: Time for a Change", Washington, D.C. May 1.

1968   "The Issue with Americans", *Solidarity,* 3(10):11-19. October.

Duff, D.F. (Lt., MC, USN) and A.R.J. (CDR., MC, USN)
1967   "Between Two Worlds: Filipinos in the U.S. Navy", *American Psychiatrist,*
        123(7):836-843. January.

Edwards, R.C., *et al.,* eds.
1972   *The Capitalist System.* Englewood Cliffs, N.J.: Prentice-Hall, Inc.

Emmanuel, J.
1983   *The Immediate and Long-Term Consequences of Nuclear War in the Philippines.* Durham,
        N.C.: Friends of the Filipino People.

Espina, M.E.
1974   "Filipinos in New Orleans", *The Proceedings of the Louisiana Academy of Sciences.* 37.

Espiritu, S.C.
1974   *A Study of the Treatment of the Philippines in Selected Social Studies Textbooks Published in the
        U.S. for the Use in Elementary and Secondary Schools.* San Francisco: R and E. Research
        Associates.

Erickson, E.H.
1966   "The Concept of Identity in Race Relations: Notes and Queries", *Daedalus,*
        94(1):145-171. Winter.

Fanon, F.
1968   *The Wretched of the Earth.* New York: Grove Press, Inc.

Finifter, A.
1975   "Emigration from the United States, An Exploratory Analysis". Paper presented at the
        Conference on Public Support for Political Systems. University of Wisconsin, Madison,
        Wisconsin. August 13-17.

Foronda, M.A., Jr.
1976   *Americans in the Heart: Ilokano Immigration to the United States (1906-1930).* Manila: De La
        Salle University Occasional Paper No. 3. August.

Foster, N.
1931-32 "Legal Status of Filipino Marriages in California", *Sociology and Social
        Research,* 60:441-454.

Fox, R.B.
1963   "Men and Women in the Philippines". In *Women in the New Asia.* Edited by B.E. Ward.
        Paris: United Nations Educational, Scientific and Cultural Organization (UNESCO). Pp.
        342-364.

1961   "The Filipino Family and Kinship", *Philippine Quarterly,* 2(1):6-9. October-December.

Fox R.B. and E.F. Flory
1974   *The Filipino People.* Manila, Philippines: The National Museum and Philippine Coast and
       Geodetic Survey.

Fox, R.B. and F. Lynch, S.J.
1956   "Ritual Co-Parenthood". In *Area Handbook on the Philippines.* Edited by University of
       Chicago Human Relations Files, Inc. Chicago: University of Chicago. Pp. 424-430.

Golley, L.1983
"For Sale: Girls", *Southeast Asia Chronicle,* 89:32. April.

Gonzalo, D.F.
1929   "Social Adjustment of Filipinos in America", *Sociology and Social Research,* 14:166-173.

Gordon, M.M.
1964   *Assimilation in America.* New York: Oxford University Press.

Gosnell, H.F.
1929   "Characteristics of the Non-Naturalized", *American Journal of Sociology,* 34(5):847-855.
       March.

1928   "Non-Naturalization: A Study in Political Assimilation", *American Journal of Sociology,*
       33(6):930-939. May.

Goulet, R. and R. Morales-Goulet
1974   *Making it in the United States: A Handbook for Filipinos.* Quezon City: Alemar-Phoenix
       Publishers.

Grunder, G.A. and W.E. Livezsey
1951   *The Philippines and the United States.* Norman, OK.: University of Oklahoma Press.

Gupta, M.L.
1973   "Outflow of High-Level Manpower from the Philippines", *International Labor Review,*
       8:167-191. February.

Guthrie, G.M. and F.A. Azores
1968   "Philippine Interpersonal Behavior Patterns", *Modernization: Its Impact in the Philippines.*
       Institute of Philippine Culture (IPC) Papers No. 6. Quezon City: Ateneo de Manila
       University Press.

Harper, E.J.
1975   *Immigration Laws of the United States.* 3rd ed. New York: Bobbs-Merrill Company.

Hartman, E.G.
1948   *The Movement to Americanize the Immigrant.* New York: Columbia University Press.

Hayner, N.S. and C.N. Reynolds
1937   "Chinese Family Lire in America", *American Sociological Review.* 2(5):630-637.

Hernandez, E.
1974   "The Makibaka Movement: A Filipino Protest and Struggle". Paper presented at the
       Conference on International Migration from the Philippines, East-West Center, Honolulu,
       Hawaii. June 10-14.

Hill, G.N. and K.T. Hill
1983   *The True Story and Analysis of the Aquino Assassination.* Sonoma, CA.: Hilltop Publishing
       Company.

Hollnsteiner, M.R.
1970   "Reciprocity in Lowland Philippines". *Four Readings on Philippine Values.* Quezon City,

Philippines: Ateneo de Manila University Press.

1969 "The Urbanization of Metropolitan Manila", *Modernization: Its Impact on the Philippines.* Institute of Philippine Culture (IPC) Papers No. 7, Quezon City: Ateneo de Manila University Press.

1963 "*The Dynamics of Power in a Philippine Municipality.* Quezon City: Community Development Research Council of the Philippines.

Hunt, C.L. and L. Lakar
1973 "Social Distance and American Policy in the Philippines", *Sociology and Social Research,* 47(4):495-509. July.

Hunt, C.L., *et al.*
1974 *Ethnic Dynamics.* Homewood, IL: The Dorsey Press.

Hutchcroft, P.
1983a "This is Whose Land?: The 'Squatter Problem' at Clark", *Southeast Asia Chronicle,* 89:20-27. April.

1983b "U.S. Bases, U.S. Bosses: Filipino Workers at Clark and Subic", *Southeast Asia Chronicle,* 89:28-31. April.

Jalee, P.
1968 *The Pillage of the Third World.* New York: Monthly Review Press.

Jayme, J.B.
1971 "Demographic and Socio-Psychological Determinants of the Migration of Filipinos to the United States". Ph. D. dissertation. Carnegie-Mellon University.

Jenks, J.
1984 "Status of Asian and Pacific Islanders in Michigan 1980". Lansing, MI: Michigan Department of Civil Rights. Research Report 18-14. June 20.

Kasperbauer, L.F.
1974 "Filipinos in Guam: An American Study". Paper presented at the Conference on International Migration from the Philippines, East-West Center, Honolulu, Hawaii. June 10-14.

Kaut, C.
1961 "Utang Na Loob: A System of Contractual Obligations Among Tagalogs", *Southwestern Journal of Anthropology,* 17(3):256-272. Autumn.

Keeley, C.B.
1972 "Philippine Migration: International Movement and Immigration to the United States", *International Migration Review,* 7(2):177-187. Summer.

1971 "Effects of the Immigration Act of 1965 on Selected Population Characteristics of Immigrants to the United States", *Demography,* 8(2):157-169. May.

Keniston, K.
1965 *The Uncommitted - Alienated Youth in American Society.* New York: Dell Publishing Co.

Kitano, H.H.
1974 *Race Relations.* Englewood Cliffs, N.J.: Prentice-Hall.

1966   "Passive Discrimination of the Normal Person", *The Journal of Social Psychology,* 70:23-31.

Konvits, M.R.
1946   "The Constitution and the Filipinos - Exclusion and Naturalization", *Common Ground,* 6:101-106. Winter.

Kroeber, A.L.
1928   *Peoples of the Philippines.* New York: American Museum of Natural History.

Landa-Jocano, F.
1974   "Stages of Adoption Among Filipino Immigrants in Hawaii". Paper presented at the Conference on International Migration from the Philippines, East-West Center, Honolulu, Hawaii. June 10-14.

1972   "Filipino Social Structure and Value System", *Siliman Journal.* 19(1):59-79. January-April.

1965   "Rethinking Filipino Cultural Heritage", *Lipunan,* 1(1).

Lasker, B.
1969   *Filipino Immigration to Continental United States and Hawaii.* New York: Arno Press and the New York Times.

Lerner, D. and M. Gorden
1969   *Eura-lantica.* Cambridge, Massachusetts: Massachusetts Institute of Technology Press.

Lynch, F.S.J.
1970   "Social Acceptance Reconsidered", *Four Readings on Philippine Values,* Quezon City: Ateneo de Manila University Press.

MacLeish, K. and D. Conger
1971   "Help for Philippine Tribes in Trouble", *National Geographic.* 140(2):220-255. August.

McWilliams, C.
1964   *Brothers Under the Skin.* Boston: Little, Brown and Company.

1939   *Factories in the Fields.* Boston: Little, Brown and Company.

Macaranas, F.M.
1984   "Filipino Americans in The United States Work Force". Paper presented at the Southeast Asian Summer Institute, Ann Arbor, Michigan. August 4, 1984.

Magdoff, H.
1972   "Militarism and Imperialism". In *The Capitalist System.* Edited by Richard C. Edwards, *et al.,* Englewood Cliffs, N.J.: Prentice-Hall, Inc. Pp. 420-426.

Majul, C.A.
1973   *Muslims in the Philippines.* Quezon City: University of the Philippines Press.

Mariano, H.
1933   "The Filipino Immigrants to the United States". M.A. Theses. University of Oregon.

Marlin, E.
1983   "Crumbs From the Military Table", *Southeast Asia Chronicle,* 89:26-27. April.

Marx, K.
1969   "Class Cohesion Through Conflict". In *Sociological Theory: A Book of Readings.* Edited by

L.A. Coser and B. Rosenberg. New York: The MacMillian Company. Pp. 206-207.

Mathews, F.H.
1970 "White Community and Yellow Peril". In *The Aliens*. Edited by L. Dinnerstein and F.C. Jaher. New York: Appleton-Century-Crofts. Pp. 268-284.

Miller, S.C.
1982 *Benevolent Assimilation*. Cambridge: Yale University Press.

Monuz, A.N.
1971 *The Filipinos in America*. Los Angeles: Mountainview Publishers, Inc.

Morales, R.F.
1974 *Makibaka: The Pilipino-American Struggle*. Los Angeles: Mountainview Publishers, Inc.

Nakpil, C.G.
1978 "The Filipino Woman in Legend and History", *Perspective Philippines,* New Year supplement of the Philippines Herald. Manila.

Nance, J.
1975 *The Gentle Tasadays*. New York:Harcourt, Brace, Javanovich.

National Board of Education (NBE)
1974 *Educational Statistics For SY 1971-72*. Manila: National Board of Education.

National Commission on Manpower Policy
1978 *Manpower and Immigration Policies in the United States*. Washington, D.C.: National Commission on Manpower Policies.

National Science Development Board (NSDB)
1976 "Enrollment in Higher Education by Level (All Schools) and by Discipline". Unpublished data. Bicuta, Rizal, Philippines: National Science Development Board.

New Republic
1942 "Unwanted Heroes", *New Republic,* Pp. 655. May 18.

Newsweek
1972 "The Philippines: The 51st State", *Newsweek,* Pp. 50-51. July 24.

1970 "They Also Served", *Newsweek,* Pp. 32-33. November 9.

Nettler, G.
1972 "The Relationships Between Attitudes and Information Concerning the Japanese in America", *American Sociological Review,* 11(2):117-119. April.

PANAMIN Foundation, Inc.
n.d. *Helping the Filipino Minorities Attain a Better Life*. Makati, Rizal, Philippines: PANAMIN Foundation, Inc.

Parel, C.P.
1974 "A Survey of Foreign-Trained Professionals in the Philippines". Paper presented at the Conference on International Migration from the Philippines, East-West Center, Honolulu, Hawaii. June 10-14.

Pena, G.
1966 "Those Filipino Oldtimers in the U.S.A.", *Weekly Nation,* 2(13):20-21. November 21.

Phelan, J.L.
1959 *The Hispanization of the Philippines: Spanish Aims and Filipino Responses*. Madison, WI:

University of Wisconsin Press.

Philippine Chronicle
1975   "The Philippine Medical Association in Chicago in Turmoil", *Philippine Chronicle*, P. 8.
       April.

Philippine Times
1975   "More Doctors Organize", *Philippine Times*. January.

_____
1974a   "Feud Costs Pinoys $185,000", *Philippine Times*. December 31.

_____
1974b   "Doctors Organize National Council", *Philippine Times*. November 30.

_____
1974c   "Youth Killed, Two Hurt in Bay Area Violence", *Philippine Times*. November 30.

_____
1974d   "Frisco Youth Gangs Bared", *Philippine Times*. August 16.

_____
1974e   "Fil-Am Group's Election in LA Spawns Legal Fight", *Philippine Times*. February 15.

_____
1974f   "Special Report", *Philippine Times*. January and February issues.

Pido, A.J.A.
1979   "A Cross-Cultural Perspective of Gender Roles: The Case of the Philippines". Paper
       presented at the North Central Sociological Association Convention, Akron, Ohio. April
       26-28.

_____
1976   "Social Structure and Immigration Process as Factors in the Analysis of a Non-White
       Immigrant Minority: The Case of the Pilipinos in Midwest City, U.S.A.". Ph. D.
       dissertation. Michigan State University.

Pilipino Development Associates, Inc.
1975   *The Pilipino Immigrants*. A 32-minute documentary motion picture on Pilipino
       immigrants to the U.S. San Jose, CA: Pilipino Development Associates, Inc.

Pinoy
1978   Special Issue on Immigration. *Pinoy*. February 20.

Pomeroy, W.J.
1974   *An American Made Tragedy*. New York: International Publishers.

Pope, J.
1968   "The Natives Who Have Not Returned", *Sunday Times Magazine*. Pp. 30-31. May 26.

Prager, J.
1972-73   "White Racial Privilege and Social Change: An Examination of the Theories of
       Racism", *Berkley Journal of Sociology*, 17:117-150.

Rahman, R.V.D.
1963   "The Negritos of the Philippines and Early Spanish Missionaries", *Studia Instituti
       Anthropos*, 18.

Recto, C.M. and R. Constantino

n.d.	*For Philippine Survival.* Durham, NC: Friends of the Filipino People.

Reich, M. and D.M. Gordon, eds.
1971	*Problems in Political Economy: An Urban Perspective.* Massachusetts: D.C. Heath and Company.

Republic of the Philippines, Department of National Defense
1952	*Advice for Officers on Temporary Duty in the U.S.* Manila: Department of National Defense.

Requiza, M.C.
1974	"The Role of Social Networks in Filipino Immigration to the East Coast of the United States". Paper presented at the Conference on International Migration from the Philippines, East-West Center, Honolulu, Hawaii. June 10-14.

Research Committee
1974	"Filipinos in Chicago: A Special Report", *Samaralan,* 1(5): December.

Rojo, T.A.
1937	"Social Maladjustment Among Filipinos in the United States", *Sociology and Social Research,* 21:447-457. May.

Salonga, J.R.
1980	"The Democratic Opposition and Its Vision of the Society Our People Want". Address delivered at the regular luncheon meeting of the Rotary Club of Manila, October 9.

Sawyer, F.H.
1900	*The Inhabitants of the Philippines.* London: Sampson, Low, Marston and Company, Ltd.

Schrimer, B.
1982	"Involuntary Suicide". Remarks made at the Anti-Nuclear Rally held in Manila, Philippines, August 11-17, 1981. Reprinted by the Friends of the Filipino People, Durham, North Carolina. July.

Shalom, S.R.
1981	*The United States and the Philippines.* Philadelphia: Institute for the Study of Human Issues, Inc.

Simmel, G.
1955	*Conflict.* Translated by K.H. Wolff. Glencoe, IL: The Free Press.

Sorel, G.
1925	*Reflections on Violence.* London: George Allen and Unwin, Ltd.

Southeast Asia Chronicle
1983	"An Unwelcome Burden: An Interview with Former Senator Jose Kiokno", *Southeast Asia Chronicle,* 89:17. April.

Spaeth, A.
1984	"Wherein Fernando Becomes Fernanda, Moves to California", *The Wall Street Journal,* 64(113):1. March 13.

Spero, S.D. and J.M. Capazzola
1973	*The Urban Community and its Bureaucracies.* New York: Dunellen Publishing Company, Inc.

State Journal
1980	"Immigrants May Fund Retirement", *State Journal.* P. A-3. March 13.

Stoodley, B.H.

1957   "Normative Attitudes of Filipino Youth Compared with German and American Youth", *American Sociological Review,* 22(5):553-560, October.

Tabb, W.K.
1971   "Race Relations Models and Social Change", *Social Problems,* 18(4):431-444, Spring.

Tan, A.S.
1972   *The Chinese in the Philippines - 1898-1935: A Study of Their National Awakening.* Quezon City: R.P. Garcia Publishing Co.

Teodoro, L.V., Jr., ed.
1983   *Out of The Struggle: The Filipinos in Hawaii.* Honolulu: University Press of Hawaii. June 29.

Tomasi, L.S.
1973   *The Ethnic Factor in the Future of Inequality.* New York: Center for Migration Studies.

UNESCO
1970   *National Science Policy and Organization of Research in the Philippines.* Science Policy Studies and Documents No. 22. Paris: United Nations Educational, Scientific and Cultural Organization.

1969   *UNESCO Statistical Yearbook 1968.* Paris, France: United Nations Educational, Scientific and Cultural Organization.

United States
1976a   "Health Professions Educational Assistance Act of 1976", (P.L. 94-484), 90 *Statutes:* 2243; *U.S. Code* Title 42, Sec. 201.

1976b   "Immigration and Nationality Act of 1976", (P.L. 94-571), 90 *Statutes:* 2703; 8 *U.S. Code* Sections 1101, 1151 et. seq.:1181-1182, 1251-1254.

1965   "Immigration and Nationality Act of 1965", (P.L. 89-236), 79 *Statutes:* 911, 8 *U.S. Code* Sec. 1151, et. seq.:1181-1182.

1952   "Immigration and Nationality Act", (P.L. 82-414), 66 *Statutes:*163; *U.S. Code:* 1101, et. seq.

1935   "An Act to Provide Means by Which Certain Filipinos Can Emigrate from the United States", 49 *Statutes:* 478-479.

U.S. Bureau of the Census
1984   "Socioeconomic Characteristics of U.S. Foreign-Born Population Detailed in Census Bureau Tabulations". Washington, D.C.: U.S. Bureau of the Census, News Release CB84-179. October 17.

1983a   *Lifetime Earnings for Men and Women in the United States: 1979.* Series P-60, No. 139. Washington, D.C.: U.S. Government Printing Office. February.

1983b   Census of Population: 1980. *PC80-1-B1 General Characteristics of the Population. United States Summary.* Washington, D.C.: U.S. Government Printing Office. May.

1983c 1980 Census of Housing. Characteristics of Housing Units, Vol. 1, Chapter A. *HC80-1-C1. General Housing Characteristics. United States Summary.* Washington, D.C.: United States Government Printing Office. May.

1983d Census of Population: 1980. *PC80-1-12. Supplementary Report. Asian and Pacific Islander by State: 1980.* Washington, D.C.: U.S. Government Printing Office. December.

1983e Census of Population: 1980. Characteristics of the Population, Vol. 1, Chapter C. *PC80-1-C1. General Social and Economic Characteristics. United States Summary.* Washington, D.C.: United States Government Printing Office. December.

1975 *Statistical Abstracts of the Untied States: 1975.* (96th ed.). Washington, D.C.: U.S. Government Printing Office.

1974 *Statistical Abstracts of the United States: 1974.* (95th ed.). Washington, D.C.: U.S. Government Printing Office.

1973a *United States Census of Population: 1970.* SUBJECT REPORTS PC(2)-1C: Persons of Spanish Origin. Washington, D.C.: U.S. Government Printing Office.

1973b *United States Census of Population: 1970.* CENSUS OF HOUSING Vol. 5, Residential Finance. Washington, D.C.: U.S. Government Printing Office.

1973c *United States Census of Population: 1970.* SUBJECT REPORTS PC(2)-1B Negro Population. Washington, D.C.: U.S. Government Printing Office.

1973d *United States Census of Population: 1970.* SUBJECT REPORTS PC(2)-1E: Japanese, Chinese and Filipinos in the United States. Washington, D.C.: U.S. Government Printing Office.

1973e *United States Census of Population: 1970.* CHARACTERISTICS OF THE POPULATION Vol. 1, Pt 1, United States Summary. Washington, D.C.: U.S. Government Printing Office.

1972 *United States Census of Population: 1970.* U.S. SUMMARY. PC(1)-C1: General Social and Economic Characteristics. Washington, D.C.: U.S. Government Printing Office.

U.S. Commission on Civil Rights
1978 *Social Indicators of Equality for Minorities and Women.* Washington, D.C.: U.S. Commission on Civil Rights.

U.S. Congress
1930 *Congressional Record.* 72(1):2734-2739. January 1.

U.S. Congress House (Committee on Foreign Affairs)
1983 *United States-Philippines Relations and the Base and Aid Agreement.* Hearings before the Subcommittee on Asian and Pacific Affairs, 98th Congress, First Session, Washington, D.C.: U.S. Government Printing Office. June 17, 23 and 28.

U.S. Congress. House. (Committee on the Judiciary).
1975 *Illegal Aliens. Hearings* before a Subcommittee on Immigration, Citizenship and
      International Law, House of Representatives on H.R. 982 and related matters,
      94th Congress, 1st Session. Washington, D.C.: U.S. Government Printing Office.

U.S. Congress. Senate. (Committee on the Judiciary)
1983 *Immigration Reform and Control.* Report on the Committee of the Judiciary on S.529 with
      Additional and Minority Views. Washington, D.C.: U.S. Government Printing Office.
      April 21.

U.S. Court/s (Eastern Michigan District)
1977 *U.S. v. Narciso. Federal Supplement,* 446:252. Washington, D.C.: U.S. Government
      Printing Office.

U.S. Department of Justice, Immigration and Naturalization Service
1976 *Annual Report.* Washington, D.C.: U.S. Government Printing Office.

_____

1975 *Annual Report.* Washington, D.C.: U.S. Government Printing Office.

_____

1971 *Annual Report.* Washington, D.C.: U.S. Government Printing Office.

_____

1970 *Annual Report.* Washington, D.C.: U.S. Government Printing Office.

_____

1966 *Annual Report.* Washington, D.C.: U.S. Government Printing Office.

_____

1965 *Annual Report.* Washington, D.C.: U.S. Government Printing Office.

_____

1961 *Annual Report.* Washington, D.C.: U.S. Government Printing Office.

_____

1960 *Annual Report.* Washington, D.C.: U.S. Government Printing Office.

U.S. Department of Labor, Bureau of Labor Statistics
1982 *Analyzing 1981 Earnings Data From the Current Survey.* Bulletin 2149.

_____

1977 *Dictionary of Occupational Titles.* Washington, D.C.: U.S. Government Printing Office.

_____

1974 *Immigrants and U.S. Labor Market.* Manpower Research Monograph No. 31.
      Washington, D.C.: U.S. Government Printing Office.

U.S. Department of State
1979 "Military Bases in the Philippines", *Treaties and Other International Acts Series 9224.*
      Washington, D.C.: U.S. Government Printing Office. January 7, Manila.

_____

1948 "Military Bases in the Philippines", *Treaties and Other International Acts Series 1775.*
      Washington, D.C.: U.S. Government Printing Office.

U.S. Immigration and Naturalization Service
1980 *1980 Statistical Yearbook of the Immigration and Naturalization Service.* Washington, D.C.:
      U.S. Government Printing Office.

U.S. President
1976   Executive Order No. 11935. "Citizenship Requirements for Federal Employment", *Federal Register,* 41(173):37301. September 3. Washington, D.C.: U.S. Government Printing Office.

U.S. Supreme Court
1973   *"Sugerman v. Dougall".* 413 U.S. *Reports:*634.

1925   *Toyota v. United States. 268 U.S. 402.* May 25.

1922   *Takao Ozawa v. United States. 260 U.S. 178.* November 15.

Useem, J. *et al.*
1963   "Men in the Middle of the Third Culture", *Human Relations,* 22:169-197.

Villarba, J.
1965   "Disunity Plagues Filipinos in the U.S.", *Examiner,* Pp. 20-30. September 12.

Waldie, J.R.
1973   "The Myth of the Ideal Minority", *Congressional Record,* 119:(3):3095-3096. Washington, D.C.: U.S. Government Printing Office.

Warrent, R. and J. Peck
1975   "Emigration from the United States: 1960-1970". Paper presented at the Annual Meeting of the Population Association of America, Seattle, Washington. April 17-19.

Weisskopf, T.E.
1972   "Capitalism and Underdevelopment". In *The Capitalist System.* Edited by R.C. Edwards, *et al.* Englewood Cliffs, N.J.: Prentice-Hall, Inc. Pp. 442-457.

Wilhelm, S.M.
1970   *Who Needs the Negro?* New York: Anchor Books.

Wingo, J.
1942   "The First Filipino Regiment", *Asia,* 42(2):562-563. October.

Wolfe, L.
1961   *Little Brown Brother.* Manila: Erehwon.

World of Work Report
1980   "Immigrants Contribute More in Texas Than They Use in Services, Says Study; Compete Initially for Low-Wage Jobs", *World of Work Report,* 5(12):83-84. December.

Yin, R.K.
1973   *Race, Creed , Color or National Origin.* Itasca, IL: F.E. Peacock Publishers, Inc.

Index